The Library Reference Series

LIBRARY HISTORY AND BIOGRAPHY

The Library Reference Series

Lee Ash
General Editor

THE UNIVERSITY
OF VIRGINIA
LIBRARY
1825-1950

Story of a
Jeffersonian Foundation

By
HARRY CLEMONS

GREGG PRESS
Boston 1972

Library of Congress Cataloging in Publication Data

Clemons, Harry, 1879-
    The University of Virginia Library, 1825-1950.

    Bibliography: p. 211-213.
    1. Virginia.   University. Library. I. Title.
[Z733.V72C57 1972]   027.7755'481   72-8477
ISBN 0-8398-0283-8

The University of Virginia Library

1825-1950

Story of a Jeffersonian Foundation

BY

Harry Clemons

LIBRARIAN 1927-1950

Foreword

BY

Dumas Malone

PROFESSOR OF HISTORY, COLUMBIA UNIVERSITY
BIOGRAPHER OF THOMAS JEFFERSON
AND EDWIN ANDERSON ALDERMAN

CHARLOTTESVILLE

UNIVERSITY OF VIRGINIA LIBRARY

1954

PRINTED IN THE UNITED STATES OF AMERICA
BY THE UNIVERSITY OF VIRGINIA PRESS

FOR JEANNIE JENKINS CLEMONS

Foreword

BY

DUMAS MALONE

THE FIRST CHAPTER of this book contains a moving description of the last visit ever made by Thomas Jefferson to the University of Virginia. It was in the April before he died that he watched, from the balcony of what is now the Colonnade Club, the raising of a capital on top of one of the pillars of the Rotunda, where for more than a century the books of the University were to have their home. Then this man of eighty-three years rode slowly back to his little mountain. Never was he privileged to see on the shelves within these walls the books that were collected according to his plans, but he was the architect and founder of the library, just as he was of the University at whose heart it lies today. For his centennial history of this University, Philip Alexander Bruce drew a theme from the saying of Emerson: "An institution is the lengthened shadow of one man." By means of an educational creation Jefferson may be said to have "institutionalized" his enthusiasm for enlightenment and his undying faith in the power of knowledge, and, as nearly as may be, to have endowed these with immortality. Likewise, in this library and its elder sister the Library of Congress, he "institutionalized" his love for books, which contain the accumulated learning and wisdom of the ages. Thus did his mortality again put on the semblance of immortality.

There is always the possibility, however, that any institution may fail of the founder's hopes, that it may become a pallid likeness of the creative personality, even that it may degenerate into a mechanism. If these dangers are to be avoided it must be perpetually revivified by other personalities, it must meet and overcome the hazards of circumstance, it must adjust itself to the conditions of changing times. As Mr. Jefferson said, the earth belongs to the living, not the dead.

Much of the present book is a story of hopes disappointed and long deferred. Following the Founder's death the library passed through a period of torpor. Nobody else seemed able to impart the same life-giving spirit, and the initial impetus was not maintained. The institution was beginning to forge forward impressively in the eighteen-fifties, but the terrible civil conflict then imposed a pause which seemed almost like death itself. The slow process of recovery was abruptly halted toward the end of the century by the fire of 1895 in the Rotunda. Most of the original books were destroyed in that catastrophe, and in the strict sense this marked the end of Jefferson's library, but there is significance in the fact that his statue was saved. The fruit of his labors might perish, but as a symbol and body of ideas he was shown to be imperishable.

The heroism and wisdom of the faculty just after the great fire of 1895 are clearly shown in the appropriate chapter of this carefully written history, and the genuine achievements of the library in the thirty years after that are generously described. But not until the first quarter of the library's second century was the Jeffersonian hope fully revived and the institution adjusted to the conditions of another age. External conditions were an important factor from 1925 to 1950, for there was extraordinary growth in the country and the University during the period; but this was also a time of depression and world war, and the graph of library progress showed a consistent upward trend even during years of adversity. The precise form that this development took is shown in the latter half of the present volume. But this is no matter of mere statistics, nor of buildings and organization. In an era of unparalleled growth again we can see the life-giving power of personality. The present institution is the lengthened shadow of another man besides the Founder. That man was the tenth librarian.

No one is so well qualified to tell the story of this quarter of a century as Harry Clemons, whose term of office began in 1927 and lasted until 1950. He fears that he may have written a subjective report instead of an objective history, and beyond a doubt this is an inside story. But to everybody who is intimately familiar with the actual developments it is obvious that he has reduced his own part in them to the absolute minimum.

The members of the present staff want to give honor where honor is most richly due, and they have drawn me into a friendly conspiracy against the historian. We hail him here as the living embodiment of the Jeffersonian tradition. In Jefferson's own country he brought that tradition to life in the twentieth century and gave it an institutional scope which not even the far-seeing Founder could have anticipated.

In view of the fact that this book contains sketches of the nine librarians of the first hundred years, an extended account of the life and career of the tenth librarian would be abundantly warranted, but it is not my purpose to give one here. It would occasion him too much embarrassment. Something should be done, however, to supplement a story that is admirable in all respects but one. As an associate of Mr. Clemons said, he did an astounding job in raising the library by its own bootstraps, while subtly arranging matters so that somebody else got the credit. Nobody can possibly read the account of the years 1925-1950 without noting the author's scrupulous effort to give full credit to everybody: the successive Presidents of the University, the

Library Committee, the staff, the major donors. Because of their number, donors stumped him somewhat in his official days, but he did everything in his power to cause every one of them to be remembered. Gift bookplates were used, so that even the casual reader would be reminded of the former owner or donor of the book. Thus, as the writer says, the library became "a storehouse of associations of affection and gratitude." One of his major fears as historian was that somebody who deserved mention and recognition would be overlooked. If anybody has been, it was certainly not his fault.

To tell the full story of a librarian who fused himself so completely with the institution he was directing would obviously require the rewriting of half of this history. It is practically impossible to distribute credit equitably in any organization, and the better the members of the staff work together the more difficult it is to determine the precise origin of policies and ideas. In this instance, however, it is safe to say that the spirit of the librarian infused the organization from top to bottom; and every reader of this story is advised to read between the lines.

Farsighted though Thomas Jefferson was, he thought of a librarian as merely a guardian of books who ought to know enough about them to give wise guidance to immature readers. By the year 1927, however, it was obvious that besides being a guard and guide the librarian of a university must be an administrator, and the persons charged with filling the vacant post in the University of Virginia concluded that professional training and experience were desirable. It was to be expected, according to Mr. Clemons, that they would, as in all previous cases, seek an alumnus. "But," as he added with a chuckle, "librarianship as a vocation appeared to have been singularly lacking in appeal to the University's graduates." Therefore, as he continues, they looked elsewhere and in their final choice they "went amusingly far afield."

They found a man in his forty-eighth year who had just been driven by the Chinese bandits from Nanking University, where he had been librarian and professor of English. He afterwards said that he had never been able to choose between these two callings and that the bandits made up his mind for him by destroying his notes. He was the first librarian of the University of Virginia to have the rank and status of a professor, nevertheless, and nobody ever doubted his fitness to move in high academic circles. He brought no notes with him out of China but he spoke the language of scholarship. He had once been reference librarian at Princeton, and it was his own idea, not that of the authorities in Virginia, that he take a refresher course in the library school of Columbia University.

If they were well informed about certain services he had rendered the American Expeditionary Force in Siberia at the end of the first World War they could not have failed to be impressed. As the representative of the American Library Association this one man in a period of a few months handled 10,000 books (plus 10 boxes, 194 parcels, 75 mail sacks, and not counting discarded magazines); he saw these through the customs (a stupendous task of disentangling red tape); he unpacked, sorted, catalogued, and repacked them. He organized more than fifty branch libraries and found time to write a series of fascinating letters in longhand, despite such minor obstacles as frozen ink. The American Library Association had the wisdom to publish these letters and one of them contained a pun which afterwards circulated in Virginia and became justly famous. While unpacking books and magazines in the frozen North the indefatigable representative of the American Library Association thought of putting this banner over the chaos: "All is not literature that litters." Harry Clemons brought the punning habit with him to a sunnier clime, and he also brought a discriminating mind.

Some have believed that he acquired in the Orient the courtly manners which so delighted the visitors to his office in later years and caused so many of them to describe him as a perfect Virginia gentleman. These comments must have tickled his funny bone whenever he heard echoes of them, for this native of Pennsylvania who had been educated in New England and New Jersey and had served heroically as a Presbyterian missionary was endowed by his Creator with an irrepressible sense of humor. When he took over his new post he looked like a rather frail man; he was clean-shaven then, and his thin face often broke into a tremendous grin. He turned out to be a delightfully humorous saint, a scholar without trace of pedantry, a courtly gentleman without tinge of pomposity, and an administrator who managed to be highly efficient and practically noiseless at the same time. Out of the wreckage of war and revolution the University of Virginia had picked up a most extraordinary bargain. He was never much of bargainer on his own account, however, and his eye was not looking for greener pastures. He had found a new home in a lovely place, he was confronting a fresh task that greatly needed to be done, and here he meant to stay.

I have always regretted that I was not present when the new librarian entered upon the service which was to engage him for a quarter of a century. Though then a member of the faculty of the University and of the Library Committee, I was on leave. When I returned, in the midst of his first academic year, I soon saw in him that unusual combination of industry and patience with statesmanlike vision which marked his entire course as an administrator. The first impression he gave was that of a man who made the best of what was available, without complaining that there was no more. For a University of high standing and distinguished history, the library was manifestly inadequate.

The collection of books was far smaller than it should have been, but it was already far too large for the quarters which had been provided by Jefferson a century before, and with necessary growth these quarters became more cramped day by day. There seemed very slight prospect of a proper building, but the librarian began to dream of one immediately and after a decade his dreams came true. Meanwhile, despising not the day of small things, he had put his house in order, consciously preparing for the great things he was sure would come. Gradually he built up a staff until at length he had one that was practically his own creation. He sent the younger members off to study methods elsewhere, but they were all infused with his own spirit of invincible friendliness and tireless service. Somehow he made even the humblest members feel that in their own places they were fully as important as he was, and that the library itself was far more important than anybody. These co-laborers were building an enduring institution.

One policy deserves special mention here, because it illustrates both the emphasis on technical effectiveness and the bold imagination of the major planner. I am referring to the adoption of the system of classification of the Library of Congress and the complete recataloguing of the existing collection of books. As a member of a subcommittee I approved the librarian's recommendation, but my predominant thought at the time was that this was a policy which I should have had neither the audacity to propose nor the patience to carry out. The story of the recataloguing enterprise is told in this book, with generous reference to everybody connected with the arduous project except the man who initiated it. Jefferson himself said, "A library in confusion loses much of its utility." There was a minimum of confusion as this supremely useful institution developed, and there appears to have been none whatever in the orderly mind that directed it.

In those days of small things, statesmanlike policies with respect to the collections themselves were worked out, and these proved important when the library became increasingly the custodian of rare books and unique manuscripts. At the modest beginnings of the collection of Virginiana, first housed in a wing of the Rotunda which was darkened by the sacred and untouchable magnolia trees, two policies emerged: (1) Such materials as the library already had were to be made accessible—not stored away in a hiding place. (2) Materials were to be collected, not in the spirit of competition with other agencies with a view to institutional advertising, but in the spirit of co-operation. This now seems a matter of common sense, since no institution can possibly maintain a monopoly of rare and unique materials and every one of them must adopt some sort of self-denying ordinance, but the collector's urge often becomes a form of madness. The library began in its own logical field, and as time went on it cultivated that intensively. Here the vision of the librarian was evident from the outset, as a single illustration will show. Even in days of exceedingly modest resources he picked up copies of the various and numerous editions of Jefferson's *Notes on Virginia,* and in the end he got them all.

It is a far cry from the old days when the Rotunda was bursting with imperfectly catalogued books, which still were far too few, to the present era of the Alderman Library, with its spacious reading rooms and its special collections of Jeffersoniana, Virginiana, and Americana which are sought out by scholars from everywhere. The collections are still inadequate for research purposes in certain areas, but in the fields which it has most emphasized, the library has become a pace-setter; and from the technical point of view it commands the admiration of all competent observers.

As one who used it in the old days and as a frequent

visitor has used it in the new, I am most disposed, however, to speak of its spirit. Long years ago Jefferson said that the main objects of all science are the freedom and happiness of man. If in the middle of the twentieth century he were to visit the library he founded, he would be enormously impressed by the card catalogues in the entrance hall and fascinated by the projectors downstairs where he could read his own letters from microfilm. But he would be most pleased, I believe, to find that the institution is no mere matter of appliances and guides and indexes, not merely an aggregation of books and manuscripts, but a living organism dedicated to the enlightenment of free human beings. He would find the Alderman Library, as thousands of students and hundreds of scholars have found it, a free and happy place. In it the riches of human knowledge are not jealously guarded by suspicious custodians, but they are gladly made available to all who seek truth and wisdom, and at every official desk there are helping hands.

The same may be said of other libraries, but there is more sunlight in this one, more warmth and courtesy and sheer human kindness, than is commonly encountered. Many have contributed to this spirit, of course, but the person most responsible for it is Harry Clemons, who with unerring instinct seized upon the best traditions of Virginia and of Jefferson and reincarnated them in an institution.

To say that is to say much, but it is to do less than justice to his distinctiveness. In his systematic labors he may have emulated the Father of the University, who always rose at dawn, but he followed a different schedule. For a number of years his twelve-hour day has been divided into two six-hour stretches. He works steadily but unhurriedly from eight till two in the daytime and from eight till two at night, varying his regimen only on Sundays, when he takes the morning off and and goes to church. I use the present tense, for his hours did not change when he retired as librarian; he has maintained them as an historian with the continued cooperation of his extraordinarily patient and understanding wife. Though the library is filled with gadgets which would delight the Founder, the tenth librarian himself clung to many old-fashioned practices. He never would dictate letters and always writes his in longhand, to be copied by a secretary or to go to friends just as they are. They are beautifully legible and his friendly correspondence has been extensive. His correspondents must be left to speak for themselves, but it can at least be said here that all his letters, and indeed all his official reports, have a literary quality, besides being spiced with wit.

In his humor he goes far beyond Thomas Jefferson and is, in fact, quite inimitable. His wit is of the *ad hoc* variety; it arises from the occasion and loses its flavor when detached from its time and place. To quote him effectively, therefore, one must reconstruct the particular circumstances. Years ago he dubbed the library department heads, who meet monthly, the Board of Aldermen and the members of it have chuckled with him over many an outrageous pun. He is a sympathetic listener to the stories of others and has an even rarer gift than wit; he makes others feel witty in his presence.

Most of all, his career and life have been marked by wisdom. In part it may be the wisdom of the immemorial East, but in the fullest and best sense it is Christian. Long ago he learned from the greatest of teachers that he who would gain his life must lose it. Selflessly losing himself in an institution which he rededicated to light and truth, he gained life and richly gave it. He transmitted a living heritage to his successors, and only those who lack faith in the values of our historic civilization can doubt that the work of his hands and their hands will be enduring.

Contents

CONTENTS

VI. 1925-1950. THE FIRST QUARTER OF THE SECOND
CENTURY

Illustrations

ILLUSTRATIONS

I

The Founding of the Library
1819-1826

THOMAS JEFFERSON was as completely the founder of the University of Virginia Library as he was the father of the University itself. The central structure of the notable group of buildings which he personally planned was designated by him for the use of the Library. The initial collection of books was selected by him, and by his efforts it was made possible to acquire the collection chiefly by purchase. Because of his wide and insatiable intellectual curiosity and of his lifetime of enthusiastic adventures as a booklover, the selection was of comprehensive scope and authoritative quality. The books were arranged for use according to his subject classification adapted from Francis Bacon. He chose the first two Librarians, and he formulated the first library regulations. During the nineteenth century there was a moderate increase in the number of volumes. But until the burning of the Rotunda in 1895, when a considerable portion of his original collection was destroyed, this was essentially Mr. Jefferson's University Library. The library materials and equipment following 1895 have been secured by the efforts of others. Yet even in this later period, there has to an accelerating degree been regard for and emphasis upon the intentions of the founder.

In establishing this Library, Jefferson adopted procedures that had become traditional in American institutions of higher learning. As was characteristic of him, the adaptations were eminently practical. That a library is an essential part of a college or university had been early and generally recognized. Harvard had started in 1636, nearly two centuries before, and among its first educational property had been 329 titles and over 400 volumes bequeathed by John Harvard. Of Yale the story is often told of the group of ministers who met at Branford, Connecticut, and each solemnly declared that he offered of his books "for the founding a College in this Colony." The University of Pennsylvania at its beginning inherited the working library of Benjamin Franklin's Academy and also the benefit of Franklin's active interest. Six years before Dartmouth acquired its charter, that college in New Hampshire had received a gift of twenty volumes from William Dickson. That there was in all cases dependence on donations for the building up of the library collections had been evident throughout the history of the earlier institutions. Thus Princeton, shortly after its opening as the College of New Jersey, gained prestige by receiving the gift of several hundred volumes from Governor Belcher of New Jersey; and during the same year that King's College, the predecessor of Columbia, was founded, it acquired "the fine library" of the Hon. Joseph Murray. It was also on record that some institutions had sent out special agents for collecting books. Eminent among these was Jeremiah Dummer, whom Yale dispatched as its colonial agent to England. Two years after the founding of Brown University, at first known as the College of Rhode Island, the Rev. Morgan Edwards went abroad to solicit books and money, carrying with him the modest sum of twenty pounds for the immediate purchase of the most needed texts. A little later the College Treasurer, John Brown, partly donated and partly raised a total of 700 pounds to be spent in books and "philosophical apparatus." Here it is to be noted that a list of the books to be acquired with that sum was prepared by President

Manning and Chancellor Hopkins, the latter being Governor of Rhode Island. As a rule, funds for the purchase of books were sorely lacking in those early days—a precedent which unfortunately became quite too firmly established. There were some curious devices for obtaining such funds. In 1734, for example, the Virginia General Assembly voted to the College of William and Mary the proceeds of a duty of a penny a gallon on imported liquors "provided that some part thereof should be spent in books." Perhaps it is not inappropriate to add that, however volatile the source of the funds might be, all the early collections were heavily weighted with tomes of deep seriousness.

These and other American Libraries were in operation long before Jefferson's University Library. The University of Virginia received its charter from the Commonwealth of Virginia in 1819, and its first session began in 1825. Previous to these dates, there had been an administrative organization for an Albemarle Academy, which in 1816 was absorbed into an administrative organization for a Central College. Neither Academy nor College reached the stage of offering instruction to students. Thomas Jefferson had been a prominent member of both organizations, and he utilized them as steps in planning for the University. Evidence of his emphasis on the importance of a library is found as early as 1814, two years before a governing body for Central College received appointment. Learning that the books of the recently deceased Joseph Priestley were about to come on the market (Jefferson had knowledge of that distinguished chemist, theologian, and political scientist through correspondence), he expressed the desirability of securing them, since they and his own extensive private collection, which he intended to donate, would together form an initial Library appropriate for the University-to-be. This early plan met with a double failure. No benefactor was forthcoming with funds for the purchase of

3

the Priestley books; and when the Library of Congress collection was destroyed by British invaders in August of that year, 1814, Jefferson felt impelled to offer his private library for acquisition by the Federal Government.

But with the University Library as with the University, Jefferson did not permit disappointments to swerve him from his goal. During the winter of 1823-1824 he helped to extract from the Virginia General Assembly a conditional appropriation of $50,000, based on the possible reimbursement by the Federal Government of state expenditures during the War of 1812. Though this was only conditional (it continued in that status during the two remaining years of Jefferson's life), he was able to persuade the University's Board of Visitors, of which he was Rector, to make advances against it for immediate use. When in April 1824 it was arranged that Francis Walker Gilmer should go to England to select members of the Faculty for the new University, upon him was also placed the responsibility to secure books and apparatus—and the sum of $6,000 was allotted for that purpose. In undertaking this mission, Gilmer was kindled with Jefferson's own enthusiasm, and he expressed "high hopes of laying the foundations of a great library." His letters of introduction gave him entree into English Universities and other learned circles, and he was able to cull much good counsel concerning booksellers and lists of essential volumes—the most impressive contribution being a long list of classical titles received from the aged critic and scholar, Dr. Samuel Parr. The London bookseller Bohn was selected as the University's English agent; and by January 1825 the first consignment of books— eight boxes of purchased volumes bearing the distinctive Bohn label—had arrived at Charlottesville.

That, however, was only a first move. Gifts for the Library had begun to come in, and in April 1825 Jefferson composed for insertion in the *Charlottesville Central Ga-*

zette and the *Richmond Enquirer* a statement concerning such gifts, so worded as to be an encouragement to other donors. Moreover he felt the need for an American agent, one who would not only supply books for the Library but who would also set up near the University a bookstore for handling texts to be used by the students. The Boston firm of Cummings, Hilliard and Company was selected, the sum of $18,000 was placed to its credit, and Jefferson undertook to supply a complete list of desirable volumes covering all fields of learning. By June 1825 this list, of nearly 7,000 volumes, had been laboriously completed. To avoid duplication, on it were checked off the titles already received from Bohn, from a catalogue compiled by the first Librarian, John Vaughan Kean. The purchases made through Cummings, Hilliard and Company began to arrive during the winter of 1825-1826. Since there had been tedious delays in the completion of the Rotunda, these books were not unpacked but were stored in the pavilion on West Lawn—now the Colonnade Club—which was being temporarily used for the Library. Jefferson's death, on 4 July 1826, denied to him the joy of seeing the University Library established in the impressive room under the dome of the Rotunda. It also denied to the University the benefit of his comments and the authority of his plans for the collection's expansion.

The actual size of the initial collection was recorded by a printed catalogue, authorized by the Faculty in December 1826 and completed by the second Librarian, William Wertenbaker, in 1828. This compilation included both purchased volumes and donations, and it followed, in somewhat modified form, the classification of the list prepared by Jefferson for the Boston book agent. The total number of volumes was slightly over 8,000.

The figure 8,000 is the one given for the University of Virginia in the list of "Colleges in the United States" in volume one—for 1830—of *The American Almanac*. Of the other libraries which have been mentioned, that list records 30,000 volumes for Harvard, 8,500 for Yale, 8,000 for Princeton, 6,000 for Brown, 3,500 for Dartmouth, and 3,400 for William and Mary, Columbia and the University of Pennsylvania not reporting. But it is at once evident that at the moment of their inception, no other college or university in the United States had thus far had available for use so large a collection of books. Thomas Jefferson's University Library was also distinctive in having special and central location and in the amount expended at the beginning for purchases. But its most remarkable feature was the effort towards authoritative coverage of all the fields of learning—and the credit for this inheres in the classified list prepared by its Founder.

On all counts that list was a remarkable achievement. It was compiled at the age of eighty-two by a man whose "active" life had been crowded with services as a lawyer, as a state legislator, as Governor of Virginia, as a member of the Continental Congress, as Minister to France, as Secretary of State, as Vice President, and as President of the United States—and a man whose correspondence and other papers are now found to fill over fifty printed volumes. The preparation was an onerous task, upon which Jefferson concentrated many hours of effort. But that effort explains only in small part the value of the compilation. As the artist Whistler testified in his famous suit against the critic Ruskin, the painting of one of his Nocturnes may have required only a day or two, but into the act went "the knowledge of a lifetime." For it was the knowledge of a lifetime that was focused upon the compilation of that list which was the foundation of Jefferson's University Library.

Jefferson's was an extremely active life, but it never lacked the friendly company of books. In an age in America which was without the modern public library, he drew on private and special collections wherever he found them. His school, college, and law training was practically a succession of four private tutors: William Douglas and James Maury, his early teachers; William Small, who was the lecturer for most of his courses at the College of William and Mary; and George Wythe, his preceptor in law. This gave him unusual access to their sizable private libraries and to their counsels on reading. The Library at the College of William and Mary contained approximately 3,000 volumes when Jefferson was a student at Williamsburg. Both in New York and in Philadelphia, and subsequently in Europe, Jefferson readily made himself familiar with existing libraries of institutions or learned societies. He took an active interest in the beginnings of the Library of Congress, which was established during his presidency, and for which he prepared a detailed statement concerning the types of books which could appropriately be selected. He also appointed the first two Librarians of Congress. In his conversations and in his correspondence, the subject of books was always congenial to him. Early in his career he began to be called upon to suggest lists of essential books and courses of reading. One such list, which he had painstakingly prepared for a young friend, was kept by him in copy and revised for reply to other later requests. Another, drawn up for Robert Skipwith in 1771, has been followed in assembling "A Virginia Gentleman's Library" which is now kept on display at Colonial Williamsburg.

He thus drew on other libraries wherever he found them. But he was himself one of the most ambitious men of his time in acquiring his own collections. He successively gathered three private libraries. His father, Peter Jefferson, had possessed a small but varied collection, with which the boy Thomas was undoubtedly familiar and to which he fell heir. The first records of his own purchases are in the

1764 day books of the office of the *Virginia Gazette* in Williamsburg. The latest is the next to the last entry, 13 June 1826, in his own account books. This covers a span of sixty-two years. Of the booksellers with whom he had dealings we have the names of over fifty. His first library was destroyed in the burning of his home at Shadwell in February 1770. He estimated the value of that collection to have been 200 pounds sterling, and he added: "Would to God it had been the money, *then* had it never cost me a sigh." At once he began the collection of a second library. Shortly before he started on his diplomatic mission in 1783, Jefferson made for his own convenience a catalogue of that collection and a list of desiderata. The catalogue and the list amounted to 2,640 volumes. It is of interest that for this catalogue of 1783, Jefferson had already adopted a subject classification based on Francis Bacon's division of the fields of knowledge as described in his *Advancement of Learning*. At the time this second collection became the National Library of the United States in 1815, Jefferson had made another catalogue of it, and the total was then 6,487 volumes—more than double the extent of the Library of Congress collection that had been burned. Jefferson then indefatigably started a third private library. This, he said, was intended for the amusement of his old age. But his conception of reading for pleasure was like Mrs. Battle's of whist: "A clear fire, a clean hearth, and the rigour of the game." Not many could unbend their minds over the tomes he gathered for this third collection. But it continued to be his purpose that books of his should be bequeathed to the University, and some of his choices from now on may well have had that intention in mind. Unfortunately the impoverishment of his estate made it seem necessary for his Executor to sell this third collection, which at the time of his death had grown to nearly a thousand volumes. It would have grieved him deeply if he had known that only three or four of his own books, which had been casually presented by him, would go to the enrichment of his University Library. But in the lifetime of preparation which went into the compilation of that list for the Boston bookdealer, Jefferson's contribution was unique.

In fairness to him, it should be stated that he himself made no claim to have taken all learning for his province. In some fields he frankly admitted that his knowledge was meagre. He was wont to seek information from others, such as George Ticknor and both James Madison, the Statesman, and his cousin of the same name, the Bishop and President of the College of William and Mary. Jefferson's list reveals both personal preference and blind spots. The library collection he selected for the University was essentially a learned library, intended for reference use to supplement what teachers and students might themselves possess. He expressly stated that it should be lumbered with nothing of mere amusement. He emphasized the importance of obtaining the best editions for each title. A book was important to Jefferson because of its usefulness, not because of its rarity. He had no little Greek, Latin, Italian, and French, and not much less Spanish. He had given special attention to Anglo-Saxon, and he himself had prepared a textbook for use in that subject. The material in English literature seems rather scanty in comparison with that from the Greek and Latin classical writers. The subjects most fully covered in his list were law, history, science, medicine, ethics and religion, belles lettres, geography, politics, and mathematics. One could expand comments on the list to considerable extent. But a better basis of judgment concerning this compiler and this compilation is afforded by Jefferson's own words—and the following single paragraph is quoted from his statement prefatory to this list prepared for Cummings, Hilliard and Company.

Some chapters are defective for the want of a more familiar

9

knowledge of their subject in the compiler, others from schisms in the science they relate to. In Medicine, e.g., the changes of theory which have successively prevailed, from the age of Hippocrates to the present day, have produced distinct schools, acting on different hypotheses, and headed by respected names, such as Stahl, Boerhave, Sydenham, Hoffman, Cullen, and our own good Dr. Rush, whose depletive and mercurial systems have formed a school, or perhaps revived that which arose on Harvey's discovery of the circulation of the blood. In Religion, divided as it is into multifarious creeds, differing in their bases, and more or less in their superstructure, such moral works have been chiefly selected as may be approved by all, omitting what is controversial and merely sectarian. Metaphysics have been incorporated with Ethics, and little extention given to them. For, while some attention may be usefully bestowed on the operations of thought, prolonged investigations of a faculty unamenable to the test of our senses, is an expense of time too unprofitable to be worthy of indulgence. Geology, too, has been merged in Mineralogy, which may properly embrace what is useful in this science, that is to say, a knowledge of the general stratification, collocation and sequence of the different species of rocks and other mineral substances, while it takes no cognisance of theories for the self-generation of the universe, or the particular revolutions of our own globe by the agency of water, fire, or other agent, subordinate to the fiat of the Creator.

The making of this list was a completed project. The task of acquiring and making accessible the works on the list was not finished in Jefferson's lifetime. By the spring of 1826 the books from the English agent had been received and largely put into use, and there were stored in the temporary library on West Lawn many boxes from the American agent, not to be opened until the Rotunda was ready for occupation. That must have been for Jefferson a vexatious delay. His last visit to the University, then in its second session, was for the purpose of viewing the library progress. The date seems to have been in April. After a conference with the Librarian, William Wertenbaker, Jefferson seated himself on the balcony before what is now the Colonnade Club, and silently observed the workmen as they raised the capital to the top of one of the pillars on the Lawn in front of the Rotunda. From the vantage point of that balcony every building that he could see was in fulfillment of his longtime dream of a University. It was a Jeffersonian dream brought into practical and symmetrical reality. His mind, gratified by this achievement, must also have teemed with plans and hopes for the future. For what had been created had vitality. After a period of meditation, he quietly went down through the first and temporary abode of the Library, mounted his horse, and rode for the last time over the familiar course from the University, this latest child of his, to his loved home on the neighboring hilltop.

II

From the Death of Thomas Jefferson to the War of 1861-1865

1826-1861

1. A TORPID INTERVAL

THOMAS JEFFERSON died on the Fourth of July 1826. Later that month the Boston bookseller, William Hilliard, with whom there had been much correspondence but whom Jefferson had never met, journeyed to Charlottesville and unpacked and checked the books which had been temporarily stored in the pavilion on West Lawn. Two months later, on September twenty-first, Edgar Allan Poe, who was a student at the University of Virginia during the second session, wrote to his foster-parent, John Allan: "They have nearly finished the Rotunda— The Pillars of the Portico are completed and it greatly improves the appearance of the whole—The books are removed into the Library—and we have a very fine collection."

The Rotunda was to continue to be the home of the general library of the University of Virginia from 1826 to 1938. This central building of the university group has received detailed and admiring study by later authorities on architecture. In his plans for the building Jefferson adapted for his purpose the design of the Emperor Hadrian's Pantheon at Rome, from plates which he found in the monumental work of the Italian architect, Andrea Palladio, editions of which were available in Italian and in English and French translations. In his interior arrangements Jefferson located the library room beneath the vaulted dome, with two floors below containing rooms for religious services and public examinations and for classes in music and drawing and similar subjects which fell outside the eight "schools" of the original curriculum. Jefferson, followed by the University of Virginia until about 1950, used "school" for what is ordinarily termed a department (as School of Ancient Languages) and "department" for what is ordinarily termed a school (as Department of Law). Later some classes of the regular "schools" outgrew the pavilions and were moved into these rooms. But the building was planned chiefly for library purposes, and it was called the Library both before the name Rotunda came into use and not infrequently thereafter. It should be admitted, however, that it was not as a library but as a public hall that the building was first used. This was in November 1824, two years before this central structure was completed—the occasion being a community dinner to the Marquis de Lafayette.

It was the Rotunda to which the attention of visitors was directed with particular pride; and from the recorded comments of some of those visitors it is evident that the guides expressed similar pride in the fact that the library collection had been selected by Jefferson. Thus in May 1831 the American naturalist and physician, Richard Harlan, noted (as stated in his volume of *Medical and Physical Researches*) that "The library, situated in the rotunda, is constructed on a large scale, and already contains many rare and valuable works, in the various departments of literature and science, principally selected by Mr. Jefferson." Some three years later, in the winter of 1834-1835, the English writer, Harriet Martineau, visited Charlottesville, and afterwards wrote, in her *Retrospect of Western Travel*, that she had surveyed "the large building, the Rotunda, and had seen the library, a well chosen collection of books, the list of which was made out by Jefferson."

But the Library had already become a going concern when the books were moved into the Rotunda. The books had been few and there had been little space for readers in the temporary quarters in the pavilion. Access to the books had been limited to one hour a day on weekdays, and on only one day a week could books be borrowed by students for outside use. Moreover each loan to students had to have the approval of a Professor. Nevertheless, the little manuscript volume of recorded loans, which has been preserved, reveals that during the first session, 1825, all but ten of the 123 students were borrowers. That was a commendable start in library service—though it may also be an early illustration of the library paradox that a high degree of circulation for outside use may merely reflect a low degree of convenience for readers within.

The Professors also were actively interested in the Library, beginning with that first session. There were seven Professors in 1825, the Professor of Law not receiving appointment until 1826. All seven took out books for themselves, and all seven participated in the signing of authorization for student loans—a responsibility which afforded opportunities not unlike those of a modern reader's adviser. Of course during the earliest years there was no code of established practices, and there was absence of the "traditions" that have come to have such social potency in institutions of higher learning. Nor was there similarity in the educational backgrounds of the members of the original Faculty. Of the seven Professors, one had been trained in Germany, three had been trained in England, one had a combined German and English training, and the two who had studied in the United States represented northern and southern environments. It was an enthusiastic and zealous group, and that spirit undoubtedly helped to establish cooperation and compliance with decisions arrived at by common counsel. But in such matters as their own use of the library materials there were occasional clashes. Professor George Blaettermann, who occupied the chair of Modern Languages, proved to be the unruly member. He was alone in claiming that keys to the library building should be supplied to Professors; he nullified a gentlemen's agreement concerning limitation of time in retaining current periodicals by first consenting and then withdrawing his signature; he protested against the fines which were consequently levied upon him; and his response to a reprimand against writing comments in the margins of library volumes was the assertion that what he wrote improved the book. But it should also be recorded of Professor Blaettermann that no one of the original Faculty except Professor Key so generously responded as he did to the requests of students for the authorization of their loans. His initials, G. B., are the only ones appearing on the loans to Edgar Allan Poe while Poe was a student.

The fact is that the original regulations of the Library as promulgated by Rector Jefferson were of the "Thou shalt not" variety; and in their formulation the effort was obviously made to anticipate such specific questions of procedure as might arise. As little as possible was left to the discretion of the Librarian. In this respect these regulations, which were adopted by the Board of Visitors 5 March 1825, indicate a practical step in the effort to put the library books in use. As in other phases of the establishment of the University, the drive toward the visioned goal had to proceed along possible routes.

Jefferson's conception of the position of Librarian seems to have combined the functions of a guide and of a guard, but not the functions of a responsible administrator. In January of that year he was thinking of the guide when he wrote to an applicant for the position that a Librarian "must ever be a man of a high order of science and able to give to enquirers an account of the character and contents of the several books under his care." In this letter he stated that the appointment of a Professor as Librarian was contemplated, who should receive a compensation of fifty dollars a year in addition to his professorial salary. Apparently none of the Professors found this proposition to his liking. Consequently the Rector then concentrated on finding a guard, to police the library room. Hence these very specific regulations (which did, indeed, retain the guide idea in requiring a Professor's presence and approval at each borrowing by a student) ; and hence, also, the inclusion of a resolution "that the salary of the Librarian be raised to the sum of 150. dollars." This, as has been noted, was early in March 1825. By the end of that month Jefferson had selected a student, John Vaughan Kean, as Librarian, and was, in the letter of appointment, admonishing him that it was his duty to protect the library property from damage, that he was to keep books and borrowers in order, and that in the strict enforcement of the regulations he was to begin with himself.

It was not an easy year for the young Librarian, a student among students. There are indications that Jefferson had overestimated the probable maturity of the young gentlemen of the University of Virginia; and in the matter of the Library, a reaction that had not been foreseen was irritation over the regulations. During the session, Kean had to seek directives from the Rector concerning objection to payment of fines and concerning the restiveness over the required presence of a Professor or of the Librarian when books were handled. With regard to Kean's presentation of the student point of view on the latter problem, Jefferson characteristically replied: "Indulgences must depend on yourself, on whom it is incumbent so to preserve the arrangement of the books under your care as never to disappoint applicants by inability to find them. A library in confusion loses much of its utility."

At this stage, therefore, the practical moves to set the Library in operation had been strict rules and the appointment of a library policeman. But Jefferson undoubtedly visualized possibilities of library service greater than these. He conceived of the guidance and administrative elements as being on the faculty level. Indeed in his own years as book collector, bibliographer, and counsellor on reading he had himself performed such service supremely well. There is a delightful glimpse at the form his vision was taking in a letter from Monticello to the Polish General Kosciusko, written in the first year after Jefferson's retirement from the presidency and Washington—a decade and a half before the first session of the University of Virginia. "A part of my occupation," he wrote, "and by no means the least pleasing, is the direction of the studies of such young men as seek it. They place themselves in the neighboring village [Charlottesville], and have use of my library and counsel, and make a part of my society. In advising the course of their reading, I endeavor to keep their attention fixed on the main objects of all science, the freedom and happiness of man. So that coming to have a share in the councils and government of their country, they will keep ever in view the sole objects of all legitimate government."

But the University had now been established; and as for its Librarian, as he acquired experience and was no longer recognized as a student, his position gradually took on increased importance. Even at the start there was one phase of the Librarian's duties which had in it the seed of future development. That was the listing of the books of which he was the guardian. In those days listing and cataloguing were regarded as synonymous terms; and before the first period of the history of the University Library was over, cataloguing had come to be recognized as a professional operation. The first Librarian, John Vaughan Kean, was early in 1825 directed to prepare a "catalogue" of the books then available in the temporary quarters in the pavilion on West Lawn. The second Librarian, William Wertenbaker, performed the clerical work for the printed catalogue of 1828, though the Faculty made the decisions concerning form. Both of these catalogues were also guides to Jefferson's classification scheme. It was expressly stipulated in the appointment letters sent by Rector Jefferson to these Librarians that they were "to keep the books . . . in their stated arrangement on the shelves according to the method and order of their Catalogue."

We have seen that Jefferson had experimented with this classification as early as 1783 when he was listing his books preparatory to going to France. He followed it in the 1815 catalogue of the collection which gave the Library of Congress a new start after the War of 1812, and which established a classification arrangement for that Library which was to prevail until 1898. He followed it again in the 1825 list for the Boston bookseller, thereby contributing to the University of Virginia Library a classification which was to continue in use until the burning of the Rotunda in 1895. Francis Bacon in his *Advancement of Learning* had proposed a philosophical division of the faculties of the mind into memory, reason, and imagination. Jefferson translated these terms into practical use for books under the general headings of history, philosophy, and the fine arts. These he had subdivided in 1783 into forty-six specific classes, in 1815 into forty-four, and in 1825 into forty-two. The variations suggest a defect which ultimately—though not for many years—led to the discarding of this system; namely, that it tended to be a forced simplification of the fields of learning, and to be both vague and inelastic. There was, indeed, still more simplification in the 1828 printed catalogue of the University of Virginia Library. This, however, may in part have been an effort to make the arrangement of the books on the shelves in the Rotunda conform to use in connection with the eight "schools." This drastic reduction was effected chiefly by crowding into a sort of catch-all twenty-ninth section entitled "Miscellaneous, including Poetry, Rhetoric, Education, &c" what had been chapters thirty-one through forty-two in the 1825 list. The 1828 Catalogue also departed from Jefferson's list by the alphabetization of the authors' names within each subdivision, by the translation into English of titles in foreign languages with an added abbreviation (e.g., Fr. for French) indicating the language of the books, and by the insertion of place and date of publication. It followed the Jefferson list in giving authors (surnames first) and number and size of volumes. The Faculty played for a time with the idea of having the cost of each book indicated, but this developed difficulties that seemed insurmountable.

It has perhaps been observed by readers of this chronicle that there exists a curious parallel between the early histories of the magnificent Library of Congress and of this modest University Library in the Commonwealth to the south. Thomas Jefferson was a potent figure in the establishment of both of these Libraries; he appointed the first two Librarians of each; each Library has developed from nucleus collections which were selected by him personally; and in the arrangement of its collections each Library followed his classification scheme practically throughout the nineteenth century.

In the founding of the University of Virginia, Jefferson combined vision with practical detail. His fundamental belief was that the preservation of free government depended on the enlightenment of the people. In planning for the University as the capstone of a general system of education for democracy he devoted himself with meticulous care to specific problems of architecture, equipment, curriculum, personnel, and administration. In their application, some of his plans had to be modified by changing conditions; and in concentration on matters of application, those who later carried on the daily details of administration sometimes failed to keep the vision. But to those who have since then striven for the broader goal of education for the nation's service, Jefferson's ideals have proved of perennial validity and vitality.

His successor as Rector of the University's Board of Visitors (from 1826 to 1834) was his long time friend James Madison, who had been throughout an associate and a consultant in the organization of the University. Madison lived at "Montpellier" near Orange Court House, some thirty miles from Charlottesville, and could make frequent trips to the University. But many of the later Rectors and members of the Board resided at a greater distance, they had perforce to be visitors in a literal sense, and increasing administrative responsibility developed for the resident Faculty and its Chairman.

So far as the Library was concerned, the Board of Visitors appointed the Librarians and appropriated the funds, while the Faculty supervised the enforcement of the regulations and selected the books to be purchased. There were, however, some uncharted areas of responsibility—such as control over the condition and use of the library building and over the classification and cataloguing of the books. Each body moved towards delegating library matters to a special committee. Such a committee, of its own members, was arranged for as early as 1827 by the Board of Visitors. But until the 1850's the Visitors' Library Committee did little except make an annual inspection in June of general conditions.

The Faculty did not use the committee method at first, but, beginning in July 1828, it experimented with having one of its members serve for a three months period as

Inspector of the Library. This practice, however, soon fell into disuse. In 1834, complaints against William Brocken-brough, who had succeeded William Wertenbaker as Librarian in 1831, were referred to a special faculty committee, and its findings, as reported to the Board of Visitors, led in 1835 to the reappointment of Wertenbaker—whose second term of service lasted from that date until 1857. The annual appointment of a Faculty Committee on the Library did not, however, begin until 1836; and its initial purpose was to approve for purchase the requests from Professors of the different "schools of instruction" and to select such general books as did not fall within the scope of a single school.

That such a committee did not come into being for ten years after the opening of the University is a sad commentary on the growth of the library collection during the first decade. The income of the University had been small. It came from a very modest annuity from the State, the tuition fees of the students, and the rental of the dormitories and the eating halls (called "hotels") —the last two sources being affected by a slow increase in enrollment. The initial expenditure for books had been comparatively large. But this now militated against the Library, giving library appropriations a low priority. Some of the orders on the list sent to the Boston bookseller had been still unfilled when the appropriation for that purchase become exhausted; and there were no funds available for the renewal of the original subscriptions to learned journals. Steps were taken towards releasing for other library use a small balance remaining from the fund used by Gilmer for the purchases in London, the employment of an English agent having been terminated. But it was July 1831 before this was accomplished. The Professors gallantly came to the rescue by subscribing personally to several of the learned journals; and at this stage there began the long series of

faculty petitions to the Visitors for annual support adequate
to continue to maintain a Library worthy of the University.
Beginning with the session of 1829-1830 there was occasional response. But for the first years the sums appropriated
ranged only from $250 to $500. This situation was prolonged by the financial depression of 1837—an early illustration of the general fact that library appropriations seem
peculiarly sensitive to tendencies toward economic retrenchment.

The fact is that, after a highly commendable start, the
Library practically stood still during the years immediately
following the death of Founder Jefferson. Even his third
private collection, which, although bequeathed to the University and after his death actually moved from Monticello
to the Rotunda, was permitted to be withdrawn and sold.
The burden of debts on his estate forced the Executor,
against his own desire, to order the sale of those books,
numbering approximately a thousand. But the sale could
have been to the University—and at least one Professor,
Robley Dunglison, in vain urged such action. That was
Jefferson's latest collection, and it contained a fair percent-
age of recent books. It was from the lack of new publications that the Library increasingly suffered. In addition to
the petitions to the Visitors, there are preserved from those
years private letters from members of the Faculty which
point with dismay to this situation. Thus Professor Lomax,
writing to John Hartwell Cocke in 1827, deplored the
"great deficiency of the modern works" and went so far as
to insist that without certain specified legal reports "instruction upon some of the most important and interesting subjects must fail." And Professor Dunglison, writing to Joseph
Carrington Cabell in 1830, vigorously asserted: "The
deficiency we feel is in new productions chiefly. The
Library is indeed in this respect in a lamentable condition.
It is utterly impossible for the Professors to keep pace with

the advancing state of Science unless the necessary materials are furnished them."

A more cheerful aspect of the situation developed from Jefferson's zeal in securing gifts for the Library. The 1828 catalogue listed books from forty-three donors—thus beginning a heart-warming story of friendly support. Throughout this first period there are scattered records of gifts. Among these, four deserve special mention—one of manuscripts, one of endowment, and two of books. Curiously enough, each of these four presented minor problems.

Thomas Jefferson was thoroughly persuaded of the value of historical records. The volumes of his own papers, which are now in the process of being edited and published, in the second half of the twentieth century, are ample proof not only of the importance of the daily productions of his pen but also of the wisdom of his insistence upon orderly preservation. The personal attention he gave to the keeping of the early minutes of the Board of Visitors and to the letters and papers connected with the beginning of the University of Virginia forms an impressive first chapter in the story of the University's collection of archives. The Board of Visitors appears to have been a little slow in following his lead, but in 1845 it took action "to have a suitable press made" for the proper preservation of such archives.

There came to the University also, probably during the first session, an important collection of manuscripts not directly connected with the history of this institution. These were the Lee Papers, presented by Richard Henry Lee, Jr., grandson of Richard Henry Lee of Revolutionary fame. The grandfather was one of the six sons of Thomas Lee of Stratford, Virginia. Two of the six were Signers of the Declaration of Independence, two were diplomats of note, and all were men of mark. These papers contained correspondence with many of the leading figures of the day. The value of the collection was realized, though somewhat dimly; and during this period sundry inchoate attempts were made to have this manuscript material carefully stored and adequately organized for research purposes.

Indeed many years were to pass before the University Library became geared to research; and in this and in the following period, the authorities were slow in granting more than a sightseer's access to the library room to any except members of the university community.

As for the first endowment for the Library, that came after the death of James Madison in 1836, in the form of a bequest of $1,500. There being no precedent for such a fund, the principal was at first simply merged with general university funds and for a time forgotten. It was not until 1852, sixteen years later, that the Library began to benefit. In the end, however, the entire income from the intervening years was restored to the Library; and this accumulation was one of the causes that made the 1850's a decade of comparative prosperity.

James Madison also bequeathed to the University Library such of his books as should not be chosen by his widow for her use. Appropriate action in acknowledgment of this bequest was taken by the Board of Visitors, but the initiative in the distribution of the books was naturally left to the famous and charming Dolley Madison (to use the spelling found on her tombstone and in several family records). She, however, took up residence in Washington in the year after the death of her husband, and "Montpellier" was left largely in the charge of John Payne Todd, her son by an earlier marriage. He lacked much of his mother's executive ability, and the matter of this bequest dragged on until it became a cause of considerable embarrassment. Finally there was resort to legal action; and in June 1854 the Librarian, William Wertenbaker, and a legal adviser of the Board of Visitors descended on "Montpellier" and collected 587 volumes.

Since that private library had benefited largely by purchases made for Madison by Jefferson when the latter was Minister to France—purchases which were especially important for the subject of constitutional law—this acquisition had an indirect association with the Founder of the Library.

So, indeed, had another gift of books which was reported to the University at about the time that Madison's bequests first became known. This was a donation from Christian Bohn, "a generous and enlightened citizen of Richmond," Virginia, a brother of the Henry Bohn of London who, with Jefferson's approval, had been chosen by Gilmer as the English agent for the Library. This was a mixed collection of several thousand items. Some of the books were duplicates of volumes already in the Rotunda, and there were a number of engravings, and some incomplete lots of unbound periodicals, mainly in German. The method used in handling this early acquisition by gift is of interest. Special committees of the Faculty were appointed to examine the material, a part of the collection was regularly shelved, a part was boxed up and stored, the engravings were put on display, and a plea, this time successful, was made to the Board of Visitors for a small appropriation for binding such periodicals as were deemed useful.

2. THE PROSPEROUS 1850's

There were several causes, in addition to the accumulation from the income of the Madison endowment, for the increased prosperity of the University of Virginia Library during the decade prior to the War of 1861-1865. The gain was mainly through advance in the enrollment figures, giving an added income from tuition fees. Economic conditions in Virginia and the other Southern States had improved; growing political tension between the South and the North tended to reduce the flow of students to northern colleges, to the benefit of the University of Virginia; railway service had penetrated to Charlottesville, opening student travel to the University to more convenient means than by stage coach; and the prestige of the University of Virginia had been enhanced by the contribution being made to secondary education by its graduates as headmasters and teachers in schools throughout this region—thereby influencing many of the graduates of those schools to continue their studies at the University. The enrollment for the session of 1856-1857, a total of 645 students, was not again equalled until the last session of the nineteenth century, 1899-1900.

This prosperous decade begat increased library activity on the part both of the Faculty and of the Board of Visitors. The addition to the curriculum of a "School" of History and General Literature (there was no School of English Literature established until 1882) stimulated the student use of the Library, and the hours of opening were gradually extended until they reached seven hours a day on weekdays. The Faculty was spurred to new efforts in requesting increases in the general book funds, and these requests now met with a moderate degree of success. The library collection had grown by about 10,000 volumes in the quarter century beginning with the first session in 1825. During the next ten years the increase was approximately 12,000. Additions were required to the shelving in the Rotunda, and at that early date the question first began to emerge as to whether the building would be adequate for library use.

Another hint of things to come appeared in emphasis on libraries of individual "schools" or of special collections, and in the suggestion that these might be located outside of the Rotunda. As early as 1837 it was permitted by the Board of Visitors that some of the medical books be moved to the Anatomical Theatre. Two years later, however, the

26

Visitors changed their minds and directed that those books be returned. In 1848 the School of Law obtained from the Visitors a special appropriation of $500 for law books—but there was no suggestion that the Law Library have a separate location. Just at the close of the period, in 1861, the recently organized Young Men's Christian Association did succeed in having some books appropriate for its purposes transferred to a reading room established at number fourteen West Lawn.

It is also of historical interest that there was early concern over the possibility of a fire in the Rotunda. A fire actually started in a cornice of the building on an early morning hour in March 1861. On that occasion, prompt action on the part of some students kept the damage at a minimum. The university community was the better able to realize its good fortune because only two years before that date the Library at the College of William and Mary had been destroyed by fire. Incidentally, there is added evidence of the expansion of the University's library resources at this time, in that the Faculty had promptly responded to the misfortune of the sister institution by making a donation of books from its duplicates. This early sign of a spirit of cooperation is also illustrated by the distribution to the other college libraries in Virginia of copies of Thomas Jefferson's *Essay Towards Facilitating Instruction in the Anglo-Saxon*, which had been published in 1851 by order of the Board of Visitors.

Likewise did the Library Committee of the Board of Visitors take on new life during this decade. For years its function had been little more than an annual inspection of the Library. Now it began to interest itself in means of bringing up to date the well-rounded collection selected by Jefferson, in emphasis on the position of Librarian, in making the library resources more readily available. Zeal for the Library animated both Visitors and Faculty—a yeasty condition, favorable for growth but also liable to germinate differences of opinion.

One such difference of opinion arose when the Visitors in June 1856 voted that a new officer be employed, "a competent Bibliographer," who should prepare a want list of important works that had been published in all fields of learning since Jefferson had compiled his notable list for the Boston bookseller. What had apparently been in the mind of the Visitors was a Thomas Jefferson II. When the Founder of the Library had made his list, the original Faculty was just being selected. But in 1856 there was an experienced Faculty in the saddle. Its members not unreasonably regarded themselves as being authorities in the learning and in the needs of their respective "Schools." The idea of calling on an outsider, however well qualified, to have authority in this selection aroused immediate antagonism. Four days after the Visitors' approval of the employment of the competent Bibliographer was announced, the Faculty assembled and protested. Its members also individually began busily to prepare lists of desiderata—with such effect that at the annual meeting of the Board a year later the proposal for the Bibliographer was quietly dropped. The Faculty had demonstrated its own proficiency. But for the Visitors also there was possibly some secret satisfaction, in having by indirections attained their actual goal.

That question at issue involved the capability of the Faculty. The possible capability of the Librarian for such an undertaking seems to have occurred to no one. Nevertheless the position of Librarian was being regarded with increased respect. William Wertenbaker had been a student when he was appointed by Jefferson, but he had long since terminated his student status. He had married and was raising a family. His annual salary had been advanced from $150 in 1826 to $600 in 1857. During its slow progress toward a competency, Wertenbaker had supplemented his income by taking on other duties. The most important of those posts was that of Secretary of the Faculty. But he had from time to time been also an assistant to the Proctor, the university postmaster, the keeper of a student "hotel," and the manager for a Richmond firm of a local bookstore, the Boston firm of Cummings and Hilliard having long since given up its agency. But in view of the accelerating growth in library resources, it was voted by the Visitors in June 1857 that the position of Librarian be separated from other posts and that in future selections of a Librarian preference should be given "to graduates [not students] of the University who were desiring to devote themselves to literary studies." At that period there seems to have been no conception of the need of special training for librarianship. To the present day protagonists in the discussions over an appropriate library school curriculum, this suggestion— "graduates . . . willing to devote themselves to literary studies"—might afford comic relief. But as a serious product of 1857, it has at least historical interest.

As for William Wertenbaker, this resulted in another interruption to his long career as University Librarian. We are not told just why he now retired. He continued to be Secretary of the Faculty, and perhaps he felt the need of a position to which could still be added other stipend producing jobs; and perhaps he could hear no clear call to devotion to literary studies. There is another aspect of the matter that may be pertinent. Both Visitors and Faculty realized that a new catalogue of the books was desirable. Wertenbaker had been the compiler of the 1828 publication, many of the books acquired since that date had passed through his hands, he had an excellent memory, and he was therefore well qualified to be a human catalogue. But possibly the Visitors and Faculty sensed the need of a service guide having less impermanence than a human catalogue; and as for Wertenbaker, it may be that the labor expended on that printed catalogue of 1828 had exhausted all inclination for a similar undertaking. These are conjectures. The facts are that a former student of the University, Thomas Berkeley Holcombe, who had demonstrated aspirations toward authorship and who had the prestige of being a brother of James Philemon Holcombe, then a Law Professor of the University of Virginia, was appointed to the position by the Board of Visitors in June 1857, to take office on September first of that year.

This action marked a definite change in the University's attitude toward the position. Except for the reappointment of Wertenbaker in 1835, this was the first time that the person chosen as Librarian had not been currently a member of the student body. It is to be noted that after the unsatisfactory experience with Brockenbrough, that practice was not continued. It was also the first time that the qualifications were not merely those of a custodian. As it turned out, however, Holcombe's case was unique in this respect until after the burning of the Rotunda. For in the succeeding appointments until that of John Shelton Patton in 1903, there was apparently no reference to devotion to literary studies.

It was not specified what form the literary studies should take, unless it was the thought of the Visitors that the preparation of "a full and accurate catalogue" met that description. For Holcombe's orders were to perform all the functions hitherto delegated to the Librarian, all those and the catalogue too. It should be remembered that this was a one man Library Staff. Moreover the comparative affluence of those few years meant a modest increase in the appropriations for book purchases, and consequently there was a corresponding increase in the amount of the routine duties connected with buying books. Furthermore all ordering of books was now to be done by him, to him was granted the privilege of suggesting titles for purchase, and he was even to be consulted by the Faculty in connection with cataloguing problems. So we find that by 1859 Holcombe was venturing to propose directly to the Faculty, and not through its Library Committee, the "propriety" of acquiring certain books and of adding certain bookcases.

With regard to the cataloguing project, the preliminary moves resembled those in the matter of the competent Bibliographer. Both had been projected by the Board of Visitors in June 1856, at which time it was ordered that a catalogue be compiled "on the plan recommended by the Smithsonian Institution." Evidently an alert Visitor had learned of the innovations introduced by Charles C. Jewett at the recently organized library of that institution in Washington. But here again there appears to have been faculty objection against the seeking of outside guidance. At any rate, in June 1857 the Board of Visitors amended its action to read that the catalogue should be compiled "on a plan to be fixed by the Faculty and reported to the Board of Visitors." With its proficiency again recognized, the Faculty proceeded with the "fixing." In October of that year it appointed a special committee to examine into the matter. The committee delegated the problem to one of its members; and by December that member, Professor Gildersleeve, had come up with a solution which found favor with both special committee and Faculty.

The Gildersleeve plan had the merit of simplicity and of being adapted to student and faculty needs. It called for entry by longhand in suitable blankbooks of an author and title list in one alphabet of all the library holdings, with bibliographic details added only for rare books; and for a separate subject index of brief entries divided under general subject classes. This time, however, the Board of Visitors did have the last word. It waited until September 1858, and then amended the "fixing" so that "in all cases the date and place of publication, the edition, and the size of the volume shall be indicated." It thus—rather sensibly it would seem —avoided the problem of decision as to what is a rare book.

This, then, was Librarian Holcombe's additional task. To it he applied himself diligently, whenever opportunity offered. The catalogue was handwritten, in folio volumes, every alternate leaf being left vacant for future accessions. He succeeded in completing the author list, in two volumes. In expressive recognition of this achievement and of his display of initiative, the Visitors in 1860 increased the Librarian's salary to $1,000.

The good times had developed slowly. With the outbreak of the war in 1861 they ended suddenly. In May of that year the library appropriation was suspended, in July the Librarian's salary was dropped to $600, and in December Holcombe was granted leave of absence for the remainder of the session. This ended Holcombe's librarianship.

The war, indeed, put an end to many of the undertakings fostered during those ten years of prosperity. Thus was terminated the first period of Jefferson's University Library after its founding. The period had covered a span of thirty-five years. There had been the beginnings of a collection of manuscripts and archives, and a single example of a library endowment fund. The book collection had grown from 8,000 to 30,000 volumes. There had been a dawning realization that to the post of Librarian could wisely be granted some measure of initiative and direct responsibility. The Library had proved of service to faculty and students; but its services had been extended very little beyond Mr. Jefferson's "academical village." Problems of extension of library equipment and of adequate cataloguing had emerged—to continue for many years as unfinished business. By 1861 both the University of Virginia and its Library had attained to positions of considerable distinction in Southern education. Both were by the War of 1861-1865 reduced to a desperate struggle for survival.

III

From the War of 1861-1865 to the Burning of the Rotunda 1861-1895

1. THE WAR

THE WAR began during the university session of 1860-1861. By that time the Faculty had increased to thirteen Professors, with five Instructors or Demonstrators; and in that session there were 604 students enrolled. None of the eight members of the original Faculty remained at the University. By contrast this Faculty was, in background and training, a more homeogeneous group. Two of the thirteen had been born abroad, and three had studied in English and German Universities. But the large majority were Southern, and seven had been students at the University of Virginia. There was a still greater sectional preponderance in the student body. Of the 604, there were 339 who came from Virginia homes; and a dozen other Southern States were represented. From north of the Potomac there were ten students from the District of Columbia, thirty from Maryland, two from Delaware, two from Pennsylvania, and one from Massachusetts. There were no foreign students, but four had made the long journey from California. Politically this academic community was composed in large part of Southern sympathizers.

33

Within this sectional loyalty there were, however, differences of opinion. The chief difference was in the attitude towards secession. The two Professors of Law, John B. Minor and James P. Holcombe, were recognized as the leading spokesmen for the opposed points of view. Professor Minor deplored the act of secession, and the majority of the Faculty were in accord with his moderate position. Professor Holcombe, however, gave voice to a more drastic attitude, and many of the students were inclined to follow Holcombe. Yet in the heated arguments in the debating societies and in articles contributed by students to the literary magazine, there was, up to this session, no lack of appeal for the preservation of the Union. But the events connected with the firing on Fort Sumter in April 1861 ended the period of debate. From that moment there was a united and extraordinary response on the part of the University of Virginia—its faculty, its students, and its alumni—in consummate and unqualified service in the cause of the Confederacy.

The expression "from that moment" is not merely rhetorical. Four days after the fall of Fort Sumter, the State of Virginia seceded. On that same day two companies of students, which had been drilling on the university grounds, received orders from Richmond, and were given leave by the Faculty, to proceed to Harper's Ferry and there take possession of a Federal arsenal. The arsenal, however, had been destroyed ere the contingent from Charlottesville arrived, and these young soldiers were sent back within a week. But one can well imagine that there were difficulties in their adjustment thereafter to classroom routines. This was within the session of 1860-1861. Immediately after the final exercises in July, a third company left for a short campaign in West Virginia. But that company, like the other two, was thereafter disbanded in order that the students could join with forces from their own home

34

localities. From that time the University's participation in the war was not in separate units but penetrated into all the military and administrative functions of the Confederate Government. The story has been nobly told in volume three of the official history of the University of Virginia by the late Philip Alexander Bruce. Poignant accounts of many of those who gave their lives are recorded in a memorial volume by John Lipscomb Johnson; and two tablets on the southern wall of the restored Rotunda silently preserve the names of nearly five hundred members of the University who made the supreme sacrifice for the Southern cause.

At the University the ending of the period of prosperity was abrupt. For the session of 1861-1862 there were only sixty-six students enrolled; and for the next three sessions the totals were forty-six, fifty, and fifty-five. These were mainly youths too young for military enlistment and, toward the close of the war, veterans whose wounds had left them incapable of further active service. Such of the Faculty as remained took on extra assignments because of Professors absent on war duties; they were themselves busily engaged in various wartime occupations; and they found it increasingly difficult to subsist on decreased salaries which, as time went on, were paid in well-nigh worthless paper script. It has been estimated that in the last wartime session the average annual faculty salary was equivalent to $31.95 in gold. But whenever the proposition emerged that the doors of the University be closed, the Faculty firmly arrayed itself in opposition. In the summer of 1862 the military authorities commandeered some of the university buildings for hospital purposes for the wounded in the campaign in the Shenandoah Valley. Beginning with the engagement at Port Republic early in June, the wounded poured in until there were some 1,400 being cared for in crowded buildings and in tents. Notwithstanding the danger of having their motives misunderstood, both Faculty and Visitors protested against the prolongation of this arrangement. It was realized that continuance by even the slenderest thread was preferable to closing of the University. In an atmosphere of anxiety, of daily emergencies, and widespread bereavements, there persisted the hope of future service.

As time went on, the buildings began to suffer from lack of repair. But they were still intact. It was not until the beginning of 1865 that the lines of actual fighting neared Charlottesville. In March of that year they swept down over Albemarle County from the Blue Ridge hills to the northwest. But the small Confederate force was then in rapid retreat; and when the Northern soldiers, under Generals Sheridan and Custer, pursued them into and past Charlottesville, a stalwart trio, composed of the Rector, the Chairman of the Faculty, and Professor Minor, met the invaders with a flag of truce and requested a guard for the university grounds. The request was courteously granted; and by constant vigilance for the next few hours, the dangers of looting and destruction were averted. By another month the articles of surrender had been signed at Appomattox. Though the University of Virginia was located at the center of a State which during those years of armed conflict had been strewn with battlefield devastation, its buildings were still standing, and within them thin classes were still receiving instruction from a weary but resolute Faculty.

What of the Library during these destructive years? Well, one is reminded of the frequently quoted reply of Sherlock Holmes to the Police Inspector in Conan Doyle's story of the "Silver Blaze." The Inspector inquired of Holmes:

> "Is there any point to which you wish to call my attention?"
> "To the curious incident of the dog in the night-time."
> "The dog did nothing in the night-time."
> "That was the curious incident."

There are two accounts of the University of Virginia during the war years by members of the Faculty who were eye-witnesses throughout. One is the journal of Socrates Maupin, Professor of Chemistry, who kept a record of the events that occurred in connection with his office as Chairman of the Faculty; the other is composed of the reminiscences contributed by Francis Henry Smith, Professor of Natural Philosophy, to the massive work on the University which was issued in two volumes in 1904. In neither is there a single mention of the Library. At least one pleasant inference may be drawn from this silence. The Library was actually in operation, though with shortened hours of opening, all through the war sessions. But in a time when difficulties were rife, the Library presented no problems that had to be met and recorded. When Thomas Holcombe departed at the end of 1861, supervision of the Library was added to the responsibilities already being borne by the Proctor, Robert Riddick Prentis. Perhaps it is not so much curious as it is creditable that during his period as Acting Librarian, 1861 to 1865, there was no barking of the dog.

The question might naturally arise as to why the appointee was not William Wertenbaker. Wertenbaker could hardly have been overlooked since he was Secretary of the Faculty, and there is no indication that he was absent from the meeting at which action was taken. But the appointment of a Librarian was a function of the Visitors, and in naming Holcombe four years before, the Visitors had been separating the posts of Librarian and Secretary of the Faculty. Therefore, in taking upon itself the emergency action of designating Proctor Prentis "to take charge of the Library until the return of Mr. Holcombe," the Faculty was less open to the accusation of usurping or contravening the authority of the Visitors than it would have been had it taken the more obvious course of placing Secretary Wertenbaker back in the library post. No further action was

37

apparently taken by either the Visitors or the Faculty; though in September 1862 the Board of Visitors did authorize its Executive Committee to employ a Librarian for the next year "whenever in their judgment it may be proper." The circumstances, financial and otherwise, being what they were, the Executive Committee seems to have decided not to disturb the existing condition.

As for the administrative duties in the Library, they were of course greatly reduced. Work on the new catalogue ceased; and as early as May 1861 appropriations for the purchase of books were suspended. In that summer, the Board of Visitors experimented with the opening of a special School of Military Science, and the Faculty voted that the Library should, for the benefit of students of that School, be kept open two hours daily during what would normally have been a vacation period. But nothing much came of that experiment. As a result of the annual inspection of the Library in July 1863, the Library Committee of the Board of Visitors reported that "The Library has every appearance of being kept with neatness, system & care, & is, we think, in good condition." As for the Rotunda itself, the committee reported that there was a serious leak in the dome. It was recommended for the following session (1863-1864) that there be a return to the original schedule of having all books borrowed or brought back within one stated hour each week. Toward the end of that session the forward-looking Faculty recommended to the Visitors that omitted library appropriations should later be made up. They also indicated their awareness of present dangers by asking the Visitors for discretionary authority to remove the books to places that should appear more safe should "incursions of the enemy" seem imminent. There was no attempt, however, to carry out such a plan during the excitement of General Sheridan's invasion of March 1865.

It is true that toward the end there was a voiced criticism of lax administration of the Library. This came from William Wertenbaker who had continued as Secretary of the Faculty, with such supplementary duties as he could accomplish. It was a complaint which revealed his dominant and laudable concern for the books which had so many years been guarded by him. He had observed that during the heat of the summer, when the University was not in session, it had been permitted that the library room be kept open. That room, protected by thick walls and rising to the curved dome, was perceptibly cooler than the neighboring buildings. To it the ladies of the Professors' families were wont to come for relaxation and companionship; and some of the war victims, who had taken refuge in the vicinity, found there an asylum during daylight hours. To Wertenbaker this meant the danger of misplaced and mutilated and missing books. The picture, however, also affords an appealing suggestion of service to a war weary community. What we do not know is the intangible effect of that storehouse of the wisdom of the past on the spirits of these frequenters, anxious and despairing over the present. There may be some shadow of excuse for the arrangement permitted by the Acting Librarian, busy elsewhere over his proctorial and other duties. He may have chosen the better part.

Before we pass on to the continuing struggle for the maintenance of the University of Virginia and its Library during the years of adjustment and reconstruction, there should be mention of a proposal made to the Faculty by George Frederick Holmes at a meeting on 1 March 1861, on the eve of the outbreak of the war. This was a preamble and set of six resolutions, ponderous in language and displaying the encylopaedic knowledge of the Professor of History and General Literature. Beginning with Thucydides, it recounted the value, proved through the ages, of the contemporary collecting of historical papers. It called for a systematic effort to assemble for a special collection, which Professor Holmes chose to name "The Memorials of the American Disruption," everything that should have a bearing on "the great political dissilience of the formerly United States of America," this collection to be zealously preserved "as a priceless and everlasting possession" and one that "would afford the only trustworthy means of ascertaining and appreciating the right, and of commemorating and censuring the wrong, which may be involved in this mighty political discussion." This was a project which would undoubtedly have received commendation from Thomas Jefferson. It did meet with the approval of this 1861 Faculty of the University of Virginia, and copies were posted widely to Federal and State officials, both North and South. A single acknowledgment was returned—from the Hon. Simon Cameron, Secretary of War in President Lincoln's Cabinet; but not one item was ever received in response to this plea. The Holmes proposal thus died of inanition—and it was at a Northern institution, the Boston Athenaeum, that a surpassingly fine Confederate collection was gathered and preserved. At the University of Virginia seventy years were to pass before, in 1930, there was to be concentration on systematic efforts to conserve and make available material in the broad fields of human relationships.

2. RECONSTRUCTION

It was a new social situation in which the University of Virginia had to operate in the period immediately following the war. There had taken place a fundamental change in the economy of the region served by the University. The comfortable life of the plantation system had been destroyed by the new labor conditions, the learned professions now faced an environment inadequate to insure their support, the discovery and development of hitherto untried natural resources was an urgent need, and it seemed indispensable that ways be found for the South to gain some share in the expanding industrialism. Education for cultural and political leadership continued to be a goal. But the immediate concern was education that would enable graduates to make a living. There was a dawning realization that this meant a change of emphasis that would place technical subjects and applied science more nearly on a par with cultural courses.

For meeting this situation, the University had several assets: a devoted and a courageous Faculty, an established organization, and a favorable reputation throughout the States that had composed the Confederacy. On the other hand, its treasury was exhausted and its source of income from the State was in a condition akin to liquidation, its buildings were in disrepair, many of the student-producing secondary schools had been closed, and most of the Southern families were sorely impoverished.

The resolute Faculty lost no time. For the first year or two its members took over the financial initiative that had hitherto been exerted by the Board of Visitors. The Professors borrowed money on their individual credit in order to have the buildings and equipment put in shape for the session of 1865-1866. Leniency was shown to veterans of the armed forces in the immediate payment of tuition fees. These prompt actions gained encouraging results in enrollment. During the 1864-1865 session there had been only fifty-five students. For 1865-1866 there was an enrollment of 258, and for 1866-1867 the number rose to 490. No small part of the reward for the Faculty was the earnest and responsive attitudes of those postwar students.

As soon as opportunity permitted, new "Schools" were added to the curriculum. In 1867 there were established a School of Applied Mathematics, the first step towards a Department of Engineering, and a School of Chemical

Technology and Agricultural Science. In 1869 the cooperation of a newly founded Miller Fund made possible the
opening of a separate School of Agriculture. Ten years
later, in 1879, there began a School of Geology; and in 1881
a School of Astronomy was organized in connection with a
donation from Leander J. McCormick which led the way
to the building and equipment of an astronomical observatory. But cultural subjects were still in the majority, and
in 1882 the School of History and General Literature was
divided into separate Schools of History and English Literature.

This expansion of subjects naturally required support
from the library collections, and for a time the Library was
but poorly equipped to meet the demands. The collection
established by Jefferson had contained some material in all
the known fields of learning. But that was in 1825. The
additions up to 1861 had been mainly in fields in which
instruction was then being given. Pleas to the Board of
Visitors for library appropriations to restore the complete
lack during 1861-1865 brought $2,000 for 1866-1867. But
this tapered down to $200 for 1872-1873, when the influ-
ence of the depression of 1873 was beginning to be felt.
The first years of the postwar period of the University
Library were like the first years after the founding, since
both were seriously handicapped by lack of funds.

Another similarity lies in the fact that in both cases
William Wertenbaker was the Librarian. The office of
Proctor had been "suspended" by the Board of Visitors,
meeting in an apprehensive mood on 6 July 1865. At that
same meeting salaries of $150 for a Librarian and $50 for
a Secretary of the Faculty were named, and the Faculty
was authorized to make the appointments. The 1857
separation of the two offices seems tacitly to have been
withdrawn. The energy displayed by the Faculty during
these critical days is revealed in this library matter. For,

The Rotunda in the 1870's

The Rotunda Annex

having evidently learned that the Visitors proposed to take this action, the Faculty went ahead and named Wertenbaker for both offices two days before the enabling act by the Board of Visitors!

So Wertenbaker, back at his original salary as Librarian, once more picked up the reins. He was able to report by June 1866 that never before had he witnessed such earnest and intelligent use of the Library by the students. By that date a more general spirit of hope pervaded the University, and the Board of Visitors advanced Wertenbaker's salary to $800. They now not only permitted him to hold additional positions but even added to the list the secretaryship of their own Board. However, when in 1871 he found it advisable to resign the post of Secretary of the Board of Visitors, his salary was dropped back to $700. Few if any books had been added to the library collection during the war, so that it now contained, as it had in 1861, something over 30,000 volumes; and there was available the two volume author list prepared by Holcombe. In view of his congeries of duties, Wertenbaker was unable to undertake the compilation of the proposed subject index. But whatever difficulties in locating books his retirement at some future time might cause, it was now fortunate that he could so well qualify as a human catalogue.

Though the appropriations for book purchase were scanty, the inflow of gifts was now resumed; and there were some new types of donors. In 1868 a visitor from New York, Abiel Abbot Low, who had made an inspection of the Library, handed Wertenbaker a cheque for five hundred dollars. Three years later he sent another cheque, of like amount. In 1873 the British Government contributed 258 volumes of the publications of the Record Office in London; and in 1874 the students in a university class in Moral Philosophy raised among themselves the sum of one hundred dollars to be used in purchasing reference works

43

in that subject. But it was a series of benefactions beginning in 1876, from William Wilson Corcoran, the Washington banker who established in the capitol city the Corcoran Art Gallery, that came like refreshing showers to those financially arid years at the University of Virginia.

The scope of the Corcoran donations may be indicated by the fact that his name has been given to the three University "Schools" of Geology, History, and Philosophy and Psychology. The gift to the Library of $5,000, $1,000 to be available for each of the five sessions from 1876 through 1881, was the smallest of the Corcoran donations, but it had an extraordinary effect on the library activities of the Faculty and the Faculty Library Committee. Lists of books needed for the new and old courses were carefully prepared and submitted to the whole Faculty and were passed upon with discrimination. In the last of the five sessions some leeway was permitted, and an attempt was made to fill in standard sets in English literature. It will be recalled that in Jefferson's original list the material from English authors seemed somewhat scanty in comparison with that from the Greek and Latin classical authors. In selecting the English writers whose works were now to be acquired in full, this Faculty—and it was a notably distinguished group—focused its judgment on individuals. For example, Fielding, Richardson, and Smollett were considered at a meeting in March 1881, and the Professors had their personal votes recorded in the minutes of the meeting. All three novelists passed this admissions test, but Fielding got in by only one vote!

Wertenbaker had amply proved himself to be a durable Librarian. But the years had been creeping up on him; and the accession of new books, purchased on the Corcoran fund, had added to his routine responsibilities. Hence it seemed advisable to Visitors and Faculty that he should have an assistant, and Frederick W. Page, who had been a student in the 1940's, was appointed to the new position

44

in 1876. This proved a happy choice; and three years later, when the aged Librarian was stricken with illness, Page was able to carry on. In 1881 Page was elected Librarian; and as an appropriate recognition of his long services, Wertenbaker was continued as Librarian Emeritus, with full salary, until his death in 1882.

At this stage in the history of the University of Virginia there was injected an unpleasant, but fortunately isolated, chapter of political control. Out of a bitter struggle over methods of handling the state debts, there arose a so-called Readjuster Party which for a short time gained supremacy in Virginia. An entirely new Board of Visitors was appointed in May 1882, and administrative officers who opposed the Readjusters, among whom was Librarian Page, were removed at the end of that session. Page did receive rather fulsome praise for his conduct of his office—but the vote of the Visitors was unanimous for a new incumbent of the post, William Aylett Winston. Winston, who had been a student during the session of 1850-1851 and later a clerk in the Virginia Legislature, was likewise appointed Secretary of the Faculty and Secretary of the Board of Visitors, and his salary was raised to $1,000—an unpalatable method of giving prestige to the librarianship by incorporating it in the spoils system.

Apparently, however, the University of Virginia possessed something of the Chinese power of assimilating a conqueror. For the new Board and the new Librarian settled down to conscientious performance of their duties; and during the four years that they remained in office there was continued growth with little outward sign of disturbance. Gifts continued to be received by the Library; and in that period there were several significant donations from outside the State. In 1882 William M. Meigs of Philadelphia contributed one hundred dollars with which to buy books in American history; in 1883 there came a library endowment bequest of $5,000 from Douglas H. Gordon of Baltimore; in 1884 Arthur W. Austin of Dedham, Massachusetts, an admirer of Thomas Jefferson, left a considerable sum for general university uses and his private collection of approximately 5,000 volumes for the Library; and in 1885 Judge William Archer Cocke of Sanford, Florida, presented one of the original copies of the first constitution of Virginia, adopted and printed in 1776. There were other gifts during those years. But these are samples of a rare book, of a general collection, of an endowment fund, and of a sum available for immediate purchase.

As a result of the state elections of 1885 the Readjuster Party went out of power, there came into being another Board of Visitors, this, however, containing some members with previous experience, and Winston was replaced as Librarian—not by Frederick Page, who had meantime become Deputy Clerk of Albemarle County, but by a former student and war veteran, James Biscoe Baker. Baker was also appointed Secretary of the Faculty, the salary slipping back to $750. Two years later Page was selected for a new office, Secretary to the Chairman of the Faculty. In 1891 there was again a regrouping of offices, the secretaryships of the Faculty and of its Chairman being combined and given to Baker, who, crippled from the war, was handicapped for the active duties of the Librarian; and Page was asked to resume the librarianship. He then continued in this office through the remainder of this postwar period and on until 1903.

What had been with apprehension anticipated in Wertenbaker's active years now came to pass; namely, the difficulty without a catalogue, human or mechanical, of locating books. The normal growth along with the Corcoran purchases and the Austin gift brought in several thousand new volumes, and the need became pressing for some sort of a finding list. The Library Committee of the Board of

Visitors sensed this need in its annual tours of inspection. But that Committee was inclined to insist that the cataloguing be done by the Librarian without extra compensation. The Library Committee of the Faculty, which was nearer to the considerable daily use of the Library, was inclined to press for a special undertaking supported by an additional appropriation. By 1891 the Faculty Committee, no longer insisting on its own capability, recommended that a member of the Faculty visit other libraries in order to observe acceptable methods of cataloguing. This recommendation appears not to have been adopted. Nevertheless knowledge of new methods was becoming current, and in 1893 there emerged a suggestion in favor of a card catalogue. This would of course involve the cataloguing of the whole collection which had now reached a total of about 53,000 volumes—not a rapid growth from the 30,000 volumes of 1861, but resulting in a haystack large enough to conceal a needle. During the session of 1894-1895 Miss Helen W. Rice, an "educated librarian," was imported from Massachusetts to begin an author catalogue on cards, and under the direction of the Faculty Library Committee the task was well started. In June 1895 the Visitors had been persuaded sufficiently to move them to appropriate $500 "to continue the card catalogue"; and in August of that year the minutes of the Board of Visitors offer a diverting sidelight by the approval of the use of $15.65 to be drawn from the regular library appropriation to enable Miss Rice's successor, Mr. R. I. Park, to pay carfare to enable him to study the systems in use in the Boston libraries. Thus this period was concluding like the previous one with definite progress in the cataloguing problem—and the new methods were also an advance over the task previously set for Thomas Holcombe.

Meantime the circulation services were expanding. The student enrollment had not yet reached the total of 1856-

1857, and the hours of opening amounted to six a day on weekdays, instead of the seven in the 1850's. But the location on the main floor of a reference collection was started in 1878, and in the following year there began experimentation with the use of books reserved for collateral reading. In 1880 plans were perfected for a summer course; and Frederick Page had inaugurated in 1878 a form of correspondence reference service.

This correspondence reference service was a step towards extending the usefulness of the University Library. The Board of Visitors was still opposed to any general policy of lending books outside of the university community —though its attitude had become somewhat relaxed in the case of nearby residents, particularly if they happened to be former members of the Board of Visitors! The Faculty was disposed to be more liberal in this matter of the use of the Library; and in such differences of opinion between these two bodies, there is a still further similarity of these years with the prewar period.

For one act of conservatism on the part of the Board of Visitors we may well be thankful. The possession of the Lee Papers continued to be a responsibility that caused uneasiness. Occasional requests were received from persons who wished to examine them, some with the intention of using the material for publication; and there was a troublesome realization that more effort should be expended in making them accessible. In 1881 a member of the Faculty suggested that they be sold to the Government of the United States for deposit in the Library of Congress, and that the money received be used for books to be designated as the Richard Henry Lee Memorial. This proposition was discussed at length. Finally by a majority vote the Faculty recommended this procedure to the Board of Visitors. But on the advice of their Library Committee the Visitors promptly expressed disapproval, stating that they believed

48

these manuscripts "to be especially appropriate & valuable to the archives of the University."

Another source for differences of opinion was in evidence through the greater part of this period—there are a score or more of references in the minutes of the Board of Visitors and of the Faculty. As between these two bodies, the conservatism in this case was, so to speak, on the other toe. For this was the lithesome theme of dancing in the Rotunda.

When social events were resumed in the decade after the war, a ball held on the evening of the final exercises of each session came to be a popular event in the graduation programme. As the years went on, student organizations arranged for "germans" on the mornings of commencement week. The conflict in opinion was as to whether these dances should be held in the library room. The Visitors were inclined to favor them, and the Faculty and Librarian Wertenbaker to be opposed. By 1890 the point at issue had reached an acute stage. When agreement was reached, it was in the nature of a compromise: that the Final Ball could continue to be held in the Rotunda, but that other dances were to be excluded from that building.

The records of these discussions maintain the usual austere tone of the official minutes. But one suspects a stray gleam or two in the eyes of these learned Professors and judicial Visitors. The otherwise consistently firm stand taken by the Faculty was in a single instance broken when in April 1892 it was a group of young ladies that petitioned for the use of the Library for a "german." The Faculty did not refer this to the Visitors, but promptly yielded, saving its face only by the conditions "that the time be limited to one o'clock, a.m., and that the expenses incurred be paid by the parties using the room." Can it possibly have any bearing that 1892 was a leap year? It may also be noted that the deft manner in which both sides used the same argument is indicative of the continued admiration for Jefferson's central building. The Visitors had argued that, since "the Annual Ball is one of the chief items of attraction for the session, it is peculiarly proper that the handsomest hall at our command should be used for the occasion." But on the question of morning dances, the Faculty voiced opposition because "by allowing such an employment of its most elegant and attractive apartment, the University sacrifices to the wishes of a few young people the advantage of exhibiting to enlightened and cultivated visitors the most interesting portion of the Institution."

This chief structure of Jefferson's architectural plan for the University of Virginia attained to an age of three score and ten years with comparatively minor ailments. The leak in the dome which was reported during the war of 1861-1865 had resulted from a prewar device of giving force to the water supply by attaching the tanks to the top of the Rotunda. Faulty construction of the tanks led to considerable damage to some of the stored library material; and after several years of tinkering, the tanks were removed. The pressing need for additional space for instructional purposes in the prosperous 1850's had also resulted in an ungainly addition, the Annex, erected just north of the Rotunda and connected with it by a portico. This was a structure which in its architectural effect would surely have grieved the Founder. In fact, a grandson of Jefferson's, Thomas Jefferson Randolph, who was at that time a member of the Board of Visitors and was later to be its Rector, criticized the Annex not only for its appearance but also for the additional fire hazard which the new building created. But this time there was no blending of practical usefulness and severe economy with beauty of design. The warning against the danger of fire was not ignored, however; and in 1886 the concern caused by a conflagration in the pavilion nearest the Rotunda on the west side resulted in the purchase of some fire equipment which was stored in a small building back of West Range.

The space gained by the Annex had been for classrooms, laboratories, and an assembly hall, not, except incidentally, for library purposes. But there was also increased need for library space. Two tendencies that were emerging in 1861 had gained marked emphasis by 1895.

It has been noted that by 1861 there had been tentative moves to transfer small groups of library material to locations outside of the Rotunda. This tendency increased during the postwar period. The student reading room for which a home had been found in 1861 was put on a more permanent basis in 1875. In 1869 a mathematics reading room was started in connection with a classroom in the Annex. In 1880 there is mention of a Professors' reading club. These were reading rooms. But it was the need of space in which to shelve the attractive Austin books that seems to have weakened such objections as there may have been to any scattering of the general library collection; and by 1886 the Board of Visitors had gone on record as willing to permit transfer of specified volumes to laboratories and Professors' classrooms. The Board was even disposed to weigh the *Congressional Record* in the balance and to find it—well, wanting storage space. Consequently by 1895 there were four separate library collections: the Astronomy Library, established in 1886 in the Leander McCormick Observatory; the Biology and Agriculture Library, transferred in 1890 to the Biological Laboratory; the Chemistry Library, separately located in 1885 in the Chemistry Laboratory west of West Range; and the Law Library, moved in 1894 to a room near the Law Department classrooms in the Annex.

As for the doubt whether the Rotunda itself, however much admired, would ultimately be adequate for the purposes of a general library, though this was but a suspicion

51

in 1861, by 1895 it had reached a distressing certainty. Space had been gained by the transfer of the four subject collections, by the addition of new shelving, and by rearrangements in the library room. But the possibility of such measures of relief appeared to be limited. By June 1894 the Faculty was ready to cut the Gordian knot by recommending first that there be an entirely new general library building and second that there be a fund for library maintenance. The amount proposed for the building fund was $50,000, to be raised by a campaign among the Alumni; and it was suggested that when the new building should be completed, the present library room be transformed into a memorial hall for the Alumni. As for the maintenance fund, it was proposed that $30,000 be taken from the portion of the Fayerweather Fund which had recently been allocated to the University of Virginia and used for the erection of new dormitories, the rentals from which should annually be applied to the purchase of books and periodicals for the Library.

With the surprising proposal that a fund be raised for a new general library building the Board of Visitors found itself in agreement; and a statement advocating such a fund and signed by the Rector of the Board and the Chairman of the Faculty was presented to the Society of the Alumni during the final exercises of 1894. That statement, however, made no mention of the maintenance fund or of the future use of the present library room; and it transferred the memorial idea to the proposed new building, which was to be called the Alumni Memorial Library, in honor of those who had fallen in the War of 1861-1865. *The Alumni Bulletin of the University of Virginia* had started publication in May of this year, and its second number, for July, broadcast the text of the statement. There was some response, the first contribution coming from the distinguished alumnus, Thomas Nelson Page. But as had happened before and was to happen again, the library project fell afoul of a general financial depression. A condition of suspended animation ensued; and though the Board of Visitors at its meeting in June 1895 offered the further proposal that there be appointed a supervising committee of nine, three from the Visitors, three from the Faculty, and three from the Alumni, which should choose an active agent to solicit subscriptions on a commission basis, the lack of enthusiastic response made it increasingly evident that the time was not ripe for such a campaign.

3. THE ROTUNDA FIRE

Such was the situation at the end of October 1895. The last Sunday of that month was clear and crisp, with a stiff breeze blowing from the Blue Ridge in the northwest. That was the direction from which the Northern soldiers had come thirty years before. They were known enemies. But of this breeze no hostile possibilities were suspected—and, in any case, no anxious group of university defenders would have ventured forth to stay the winds.

Mr. Jefferson's University Library, now grown from 8,000 to over 56,000 volumes, was for the most part in the Rotunda. Jutting northward from that original circular building was the Annex, a rectangular structure of three stories and a basement, approximately one hundred by fifty feet in dimensions, its plain exterior adorned with pillars at each end, the pillars at the south end supporting an extension of its roof line to the circular band beneath the Rotunda dome. Four years before this date, the Chapel west of the Annex had been completed. Between these two buildings and reaching towards the road in front of the university grounds was "the pond"—a small sheet of shallow water.

This was the familiar scene which met the eyes of a student, Mason Foshee, who was leisurely returning from a late Sunday morning breakfast. But not familiar were the whiffs of smoke curling out from the eaves at the northern end of the Annex and whipped back by the breeze. After a moment of uncomprehending wonderment, Foshee called to two other students who were nearby, and all three with shouts of "Fire!" dashed off to find old Henry Martin, the janitor and bell ringer. Uncle Henry was soon located, and he began the violent ringing of the college bell, at that time suspended in the south portico of the Rotunda. The students, their numbers rapidly increased, sped on to the fire house behind West Range. Breaking open the door, they manned the ropes and pulled the diminutive equipment to the edge of the pond. There was no suction pump, however; and the best that could be done was to attach the hose to a fire plug north of the Annex, and to rely on the meagre force which the hydrant stream would yield. It was soon evident that the moment had passed for the fire to be extinguished by such means, and the fast growing crowd turned its efforts to the saving of the contents of the building. Led by action rather than command, excited groups rescued much detached equipment, particularly from the lower parts of the Annex. One such group, with which was Raleigh Minor, Professor of Law, carried to safety practically the whole law library collection.

Meantime the flames, aided along the roof by the wind, were sweeping towards the Rotunda. William Echols, who in addition to being Adjunct Professor of Applied Mathematics was in charge of buildings and grounds, had begun a series of efforts to blast away with dynamite the connection between the Annex and the Rotunda, efforts which marked him as the outstanding hero of a day replete with daring deeds. The pillars supporting the extension of the roof between the two structures were shattered. But the roof did not fall; and along it leaped the now raging fire into the gallery circling above the general library room.

54

Within the Rotunda the rescue squads, a toiling medley of professors, students, ladies clad in their Sunday best, and citizens who had hurried away from the church services in Charlottesville, were strenuously carrying out whatever seemed movable. It was a pandemonium of shouted directions, breaking glass, falling timbers, and stifling smoke, the whole scene lighted horribly by spurts of yellow flame from the gallery above. Yet in the seemingly utter confusion there was evidence of ready skill linked with well-nigh superhuman strength. Such was the removal from its base and down the narrow circular stairway of the Alexander Galt statue of Jefferson—seven feet high and of solid marble. The portraits that had adorned the library room had been laboriously carried out and left on the Lawn, to gaze blankly at the sky or from queer angles at this strange outdoors. Thousands of the books on the main floor, many of them reference books, were borne in unwieldy armfuls and dropped in disorderly piles on the grass. Some were pitched out from the windows above, and caught in sheets stretched below. But of what was in the gallery little could be saved. From the very start the flames had outsped the efforts to stay them or to salvage their prey; and now orders had to be given forbidding further entrance into the Rotunda.

It had indeed become necessary to give attention to the two wings that linked the Rotunda with the pavilions on East and West Lawn—at that period there were no parallel wings extending from the northern part of the Rotunda. One of these southern wings, that reaching toward West Lawn, also contained library material, the periodicals and books of the students' reading room. The effort now was to demolish these wings; and the pavilions beyond were being covered with blankets drenched by a rapidly organized bucket and pitcher brigade—when suddenly the hostile wind turned friendly and veered, to blow from the southward. Meanwhile telegrams had brought fire equipment from Staunton and Lynchburg, and more was on its way from Richmond. The weary fire fighters now had their chance to turn the tide of battle—and by early afternoon the conflagration was under control.

But it was a different scene from that which had been leisurely viewed by Student Foshee a few hours before. The Annex had been gutted, one wall had fallen, and the others were visibly tottering. The dome of the Rotunda had crashed in; and inside the circular walls was a smoking mass from which fitful flames arose as from the crater of a smouldering volcano. But the stout walls were firmly standing, and on the lawn side the six tall pillars, which Jefferson had viewed on his last visit to the University, were still erect. Scattered among the piles of books heaped upon the grass there were only a few hundred of the volumes which Jefferson had originally chosen. But resting safely on mattresses snatched by students from their beds was the Jefferson statue, prone for the moment, but undamaged save for a small crack in the formal drapery.

A few weeks before this October Sunday, Librarian Page had written for the *Alumni Bulletin* the story of the founding of the University Library and of its more recent history. That day the news of the fire had not reached him until late in its course. He hurried up the hill of the Rotunda, with mounting dismay as he neared the appalling scene. When he peered in at the familiar entrance, further attempts at salvage had been forbidden. This home of his later years— in the next month he would pass his sixty-ninth birthday— where his orderly habits and his love of books had brought him daily joy in service, was an inferno. What in his historical article he had affectionately termed "Our Library" was now a reality of the past. The present was a terrifying nightmare. Death had been merciful to William Wertenbaker. But to Frederick Page, here was stark tragedy.

IV

From the Burning of the Rotunda to the End of the Library's First Century---1895-1925

1. AFTERMATH OF THE FIRE

THE BURNING of the Rotunda was tragedy for the whole University. Yet the fable of the phoenix has seldom been more appropriately applied than to the events which directly followed. As soon as there was confidence that further spread of the fire could be prevented, the Chairman, William Mynn Thornton, summoned the Faculty to a meeting in the Chemical Laboratory. This was at three o'clock. Wilson Cary Nicholas Randolph, the Rector of the Board of Visitors and a great grandson of Thomas Jefferson, and Armistead Churchill Gordon, a member of the Board who was later to be its Rector, were on the scene and attended the meeting. Actions were promptly taken to delegate authority for the procedures that were immediately necessary, and a new room schedule was devised for the Monday morning classes. There were no longer a Rotunda clock and a college bell. But the classes met promptly, and there was admirable concentration on the subject matter of the courses. Four days later, on Thursday of that week, the Faculty had completed for recommendation to the Board of Visitors a reconstruction programme which for comprehensiveness, foresight, and attention to practical detail is undoubtedly the peer of any document ever prepared by the University of Virginia Faculty. There had been courage and forcefulness in the faculty actions at the close of the War of 1861-1865. But it can be affirmed that what followed the Rotunda fire was for the Faculty "their finest hour."

When the Board of Visitors assembled, it approved with little change the recommendations of the Faculty, and a joint committee from these two bodies was appointed to carry out the building programme. It was resolved that the Annex should not be rebuilt, that the restored Rotunda and the new buildings that were proposed should be of fire resisting construction and should follow Jefferson's architectural patterns, and that an outstanding architect should be secured for this purpose. There has been general agreement that Stanford White was an excellent choice.

It is true that in planning for the restoration of the Rotunda, the lesson that had been learned concerning the probable inadequacy of that building for the purposes of a library was largely forgotten. There did come, indeed, from the Richmond Alumni a reminder of the arguments that had been advanced only a few months before in advocating the project of a new building. But it was now felt that the all embracing need was for restoration funds; and in the plans for rebuilding the Rotunda there emerged possibilities for a considerable extension of the space for library purposes. In the circumstances, the restoration of the Rotunda as the Library was probably the better immediate solution. Those recent proposals for a new building had shown little realization of the library requirements involved in university research. The erection at that time of a new building scaled merely to college library size might seriously have complicated and delayed the later effort to secure a more adequately conceived university library building and equipment.

58

Burning of the Rotunda

The Rotunda Library Room before the fire (upper)
and about 1920, after restoration (lower)

There was considerable debate over permitting any change from the interior plan of the original Rotunda. But the final decision was to eliminate the upper floor and to place the floor of the circular library room on the level of the entrance from the portico, with three galleries above, the top gallery being open, guarded on the inside by merely a low railing. Below the main floor, on the level of the ground entrance, were two oval rooms, the passage way between following the lines of the oval rooms, thus being shaped somewhat like an hourglass. The wings extending from the Rotunda base to the first pavilions on East and West Lawn were restored; and this time parallel wings were constructed from the northern base of the Rotunda. The general library collection was to be returned to the enlarged library room, and the law library collection to be located in the two oval rooms beneath. The four wings might temporarily be used for other purposes but could later be made available for library use if the need should arise. Faults that developed in some of the concrete work done at that period made necessary certain repairs in 1939 and 1940, after the library collections had finally been moved to a new building. But these later repairs did not materially alter the interior plan, and the Rotunda of the restoration after the fire is essentially the Rotunda of the present day.

As for the collection of books, specific figures are given in the accounts contemporary with the fire. It is stated that on the morning of that October Sunday there were 56,733 volumes in the University Library and that on the evening of that selfsame day there were 17,194. The increase from the 8,000 of the original library to 56,733 in 1895 had been comparatively slow. All of the eight university or college libraries mentioned in connection with the founding of the University of Virginia Library were well above 56,733 volumes in 1895, with the exception of the Library at the College of William and Mary, which had been destroyed by fire in 1859 and had suffered from the closing of that college in 1861-1865 and in 1881-1888. For the annual report of the United States Commissioner of Education for the session ending with June 1895 Harvard had supplied a figure of 452,512 volumes, Yale of 220,000, Columbia of 200,000, Princeton of 171,000, and Pennsylvania of 120,000. By that date eight other university libraries had collections larger than that at the University of Virginia, the leaders being Chicago with 300,000, Cornell with 173,450, and Wisconsin with 135,000. But what had been a gradual decline in comparative size during the seventy years since the founding by Thomas Jefferson became a plummeted fall in the few hours of the fire. By that year's record of the Federal Commissioner of Education it was a fall, in number of volumes among university and college libraries, from sixteenth place to seventy-seventh place.

Of course the number of volumes affords only a partial standard for ranking libraries. Two collections having the same totals may differ widely in availability for use, in suitability for local needs, and in quality and distinction. By those tests, the fall of the University of Virginia Library was probably far below seventy-seventh place.

By the test of availability, Jefferson's generalization to Librarian Kean in 1825—"A library in confusion loses much of its utility"—would now have particular application. This had become not a working but an unworkable collection, and its emergence out of that condition was distressingly slow. The books piled on the Lawn were, as soon as arrangements could be made, moved to temporary shelves on an upper floor of the Brooks Museum, a structure of eccentric architectural design located on the slope northeast of the Rotunda site. There in a crowded and confused state the books had to remain for three years, until

November 1898. Even after they were returned to the restored library room, the shelving of the books continued to be of the helter-skelter variety. Moreover there were no finding lists. The author card catalogue had indeed been saved. But that was now merely an instrument of tantalization, constantly offering reminders of volumes that had been destroyed in the flames.

By the test of suitability for local needs, the surviving collection had also fallen low in the scale. Much of the growth of the Library during its seventy years had been in books dealing with the subjects of the various "Schools" into which the curriculum was divided. Fortunately some of the most frequently used books had been on the main floor of the library room, and a considerable number of those had been saved. But those did not include material for all of the "Schools." The medical collection, for example, had been located in the gallery, and it was reported to have been totally destroyed. Moreover what had been salvaged in general afforded but meagre support for the resumption of university courses on the scale maintained before the fire. The Faculty now had bitter confirmation of their assertions through the years that an adequate library collection was essential for instruction by university standards.

By the test of quality and distinction the loss was indeed tragic. The collection created by the Founder had a unique character that was quite lacking in the beginnings of the present University of Virginia Library. The original collection had not been composed of rare books, but of books selected as being the best in their fields. By 1895 some of them had also become rare books. The impressive feature of that selection had been that it was an authoritative attempt to cover all departments of learning. In that respect the 8,000 volumes of the 1828 Catalogue were far superior to the 17,194 salvaged from the fire.

It is by a comparison between the 1825 and the 1895 situations that Thomas Jefferson's achievement can be more adequately realized. It will be recalled that Jefferson personally prepared the master list for the original collection, that he found the money to purchase the books on that list, that he insured accessibility by his subject classification, and that he pleaded for gifts to supplement his compact nucleus collection. These four methods do not tell the whole story. But they will suffice for the purpose of this comparison.

In only the last of the four, the solicitation for gifts, was the success in 1895 and the years following greater than at the founding of the Library. At this point the University in 1895 had an outstanding advantage. In Jefferson's day there were friends of the University, but there were no alumni. The 1828 Catalogue lists a creditable number of donations. But the response to the solicitation for gifts after the burning of the Rotunda was extraordinary, and it continued for many years. Indeed that success is, as we shall see, the main theme of the Library's story from 1895 to 1925.

Not so with the other three methods. In the matter of the classification there was to be a complete—and justifiable—break with the Jefferson-Bacon system of 1825. But for the first decade there was for the new collection very little of any system. There was no master list to give comprehensiveness to the new collection; and the immediate story of funds appropriated for the purchase of books is an uncomfortably near approach to the famous chapter on the snakes in Ireland.

Here, unfortunately, was the crux of the 1895 situation. With an able Faculty, such as this one was, it is probable that much could have been done toward the compilation of a master list. But with the heavy additional burden of reconstruction tasks upon them, there was need of the encouragement of visible funds before the attempt be undertaken. Jefferson had devised a way to extract $50,000 for books and equipment, and before his death more than half of that amount had been drawn on for the purchase of books from his 1825 list. On 31 October 1895, four days after the fire, the Faculty, in a letter of appeal for the new library collection, named that same amount, $50,000, as needed for immediate purchase of books, with another $50,000 as endowment. But the generous response that ensued followed the law of the superior attraction of specific objects. A large majority of the donations consisted of books. There were also in the next five years four that involved money; but these, the subscriptions for the Hertz and Holmes books and the Byrd and D'Arcy Paul endowment funds, were restricted as to use. Apparently no general funds were received.

What of general appropriations? When the Faculty Editors compiled the University Catalogue for 1896-1897, those Editors displayed courageous optimism in a footnote which read: "It is expected that liberal money appropriation will be made by the Visitors toward the speedy restoration of the Library." Two years later this was even more hopefully revised to read: "It is confidently expected . . . that in the near future . . ." Yet that footnote ran regularly through seven annual issues; and its disappearance after the catalogue for 1902-1903 may have been merely in realization that the impending election of a President of the University would shift the target for such requests.

Of course there were possible arguments against much buying of books. Gifts of books were beginning to arrive in seeming abundance. Why not, therefore, wait to see if among them were not some of the needed volumes? Hence, except for small grants to the Law Library, during this decade the book appropriations were mainly limited to the annual income of $456 from the Madison and Gordon endowments; and when later the Byrd and D'Arcy Paul endowments increased the total to $948, the use of the two new funds was, as has been stated, restricted to certain types of expenditure.

It is also easy to understand that after the fire in 1895 all available finances were being absorbed into the building programme. That programme included other buildings than the Rotunda. But the Rotunda was the most expensive, and it was for library use. Moreover there were already more than seventeen thousand books. It might therefore appear reasonable that any expenditure for books be omitted—or at least postponed. Here again the parallel with 1825 makes Jefferson's performance the more remarkable. Then also there was an all pervasive programme for building construction. It included both the Rotunda and other needed buildings; and Jefferson's own third collection and other gifts could be counted on for the Library. Nevertheless, in the midst of those very circumstances, Jefferson had insisted that general funds for purchase of a comprehensive collection were a first essential—and he got them. In 1825 Jefferson achieved by purchase a nucleus library superior to that of any other previous American college or university at its beginning. In 1895 the Faculty was, as it were, a voice crying in a wilderness of building materials.

Much more pleasant is the story of the use by the Faculty of the Jefferson precedent for the solicitation of gifts. The letter of appeal to Alumni and Friends of the University was ready on the same day that the Faculty's reconstruction programme was forwarded to the Board of Visitors; and the resident Chaplain for the session of 1895-1896, the Rev. John William Jones, undertook the task of sending it out widely. The response was heart-warming. Books poured in, not only from individuals and groups of individuals but also from other institutions and from publishers. The inflow continued in such abundance that the University Catalogue for the session of 1904-1905 could announce that the library collection then contained "more than sixty thousand volumes." Hence in this second beginning, the Library had in ten years increased to a total in excess of the figure, 56,733 volumes, it had previously reached in seventy years. It is not clear what proportion of the sixty thousand had been made available for use; and coming from a multitude of donors, it was unavoidable that in some fields there should be a large degree of duplication and in others a paucity of material. This library phoenix that arose from the ashes was a scion of large wingspread, but its body lacked the compact symmetry of its predecessor.

In the rapid increase there were a number of noteworthy collections. Mention of a few of these will illustrate the types of the acquisitions during the first decade after the fire. By the prompt and generous action of the Alumni Association of New York City, the classical library of the German scholar, Martin Julius Hertz, which had just come on the market (Professor Hertz died 22 September 1895), was purchased and presented to the University of Virginia. There were approximately 12,000 books and 3,000 pamphlets and programmes in that collection. A prime mover in this effective response to the needs of the Library was Thomas Randolph Price, a Professor at Columbia University, who had from 1876 to 1882 been Professor of Greek at the University of Virginia, succeeding Professor Gildersleeve in that post. Professor Price's own private library, largely classical and comprising about 4,000 volumes, was after his death in 1903 presented by his widow and his daughter. The private collection of another Professor, George Frederick Holmes (he had been a member of the Faculty from 1857 until his death in 1897) was also secured for the University Library, in this case largely through subscriptions from his former students. The cheque completing the amount necessary for this purchase came from William Andrews Clark, this being the first of a notable series of his contributions. Still another Professor, James Albert Harrison, who between 1895 and 1911 gave a striking example of versatility by occupying successively chairs of English, Romance Languages, and Teutonic Languages, inaugurated by personal gifts a collection of Southern authors, with special emphasis on Edgar Allan Poe. Among the many valuable donations by Alumni were the extensive private library, approximately 5,000 volumes, of Frederick William Markey Holliday, who had been Governor of Virginia from 1878 to 1882, and a series of gifts of choice works on bibliography, botany, theology, and other subjects from the Rev. Haslett McKim. From one who was neither a Professor nor an Alumnus, but who proved himself to be a true friend of the University of Virginia, came a collection of between two and three thousand volumes on Southern history and development. This donor was Barnard Shipp, a native of Mississippi and for many years a resident of Louisville, Kentucky. Both the Law Library and the Medical Library were enriched by gifts during this decade: the Law Library by the law books of General Bradley Tyler Johnson, presented by his son, who was a law graduate of the University of Virginia, and by a collection donated by Judge Lambert Tree, an Alumnus of the Department of Law; and the Medical Library by medical works which had belonged to James Bolton, presented by his son who was an Alumnus, and by a collection which had been the private library of a Medical Alumnus, James L. Leitch, this being donated by his widow. During this decade there was continued the annual solicitation for gifts and exchanges of astronomical publications which had been started by Ormond Stone, Professor of Astronomy, in 1886. The accumulated results of this annual programme were to result in making the Astronomy Library, located at the Leander McCormick Observatory, outstanding in the South. There were also two additions to the endowment funds, both received in

1899. The first was in memory of D'Arcy Paul, who had been a law student during the sessions 1877-1879. This fund, given by his widow, amounted to $1,000, and the income was to be used for the purchase of periodicals in Modern Languages. The second was the estate of Alfred Henry Byrd, a college student during the sessions 1885-1888. This amounted to $10,180, and the income was to be used for the purchase of Virginiana.

This latter fund was instrumental in opening the way for emphasis on research. So far the University Library had been administered with an eye single to its service as a college library. It is true that in the possession of the Lee Papers, which had survived the fire, there had inhered in the library collection since its beginning in 1825 the possibilities of research; and that the recognized failure to develop those possibilities adequately had at times weighed on the consciences of the Faculty and Visitors. But when the annual income from the Byrd Fund became available about 1900, a new kind of responsibility emerged—the responsibility of continuing selection and acquisition of historical, literary, and social material not immediately connected with the undergraduate curriculum. The conception of a research library did not, like the Goddess of Wisdom, spring full-grown from a Jovian headache. The headache was to prove rather to be in the nature of a chronic migraine. But from its beginning the Byrd Fund offered the possibility of an extension of the library services.

The books had begun to arrive in quantity while the Library was still located in congested quarters in the Brooks Museum, and both faculty and students grew impatient over delays in completing and equipping the new library room in the restored Rotunda. In the three sessions from 1895 to 1898, library service was limited to the lending of such books as could be located; use of the Library for reading and study was practically eliminated; and there was natural curiosity over the contents of the unopened boxes of gifts. When the move back to the Rotunda did take place in November 1898, it was performed by willing students, under the direction of the Chairman of the Faculty Library Committee and the Librarian, with an excitement akin to that of the rescue efforts during the fire—only this was a glad excitement.

In the new library room both the seating and the shelving arrangements were insufficient for a number of years; and the handling of the gift acquisitions was like clearing pavements during a snowstorm. But as soon as the books were again in the Rotunda, the use of the Library mounted. The daily hours of opening, excluding Sundays, were expanded from six to ten, and the recorded circulation for the session of 1901-1902 had already reached a higher total than in 1894-1895, the year before the fire. Meantime an increased interest in the University of Virginia, which, in part at least, was a salutary effect of the disaster of 1895, had been accompanied by larger enrollments, until the total for 1899-1900, namely 664 students, for the first time exceeded the previous high point, 645, attained back in 1856-1857.

With this increase in student readers and in hours of opening, Librarian Page had little opportunity to give time to cataloguing. He devoted himself with patient zeal and unfailing courtesy to guidance in reading and to searching the shelves for needed books. He was wont to allow trusted students to do their own searching—a time-consuming but often a profitable experience for them. This freedom was far different from the strict control of all student readers during the first years of the Library's history. Perhaps Frederick Page's greatest contribution was his demonstration that the spirit of the service could be maintained even in the absence of the library techniques.

But with the appointment of the next Librarian there

began to be consideration of techniques. At least there was a nearer approach to emphasis on professional qualifications than had been in evidence since the selection of Thomas Holcombe in the years just prior to 1861. In the choice of John Shelton Patton to succeed Frederick Page in 1903, what was in demand was, it is true, not professional status in the present-day understanding of that term. There was apparently some consideration of the qualification that had prevailed in the selection of Holcombe, namely, devotion to literary studies; and Patton, who had been a newspaper reporter and editor, and had "proceeded author" by the compilation of a handbook of the University of Virginia in 1900, had supplied proof of such devotion. But the confused condition that had prevailed since the Rotunda fire showed the need of someone with organizational and executive experience. Patton could not offer this as far as library service was concerned. However in civic affairs he had risen to be Mayor of Charlottesville, and in educational affairs to be Superintendent of Schools; and it appeared reasonable to believe that there could be a ready transfer of executive ability to the library field. What was possibly a determining factor in the appointment was Patton's own desire for the position. By 1902 there seemed little doubt that there was to be a radical change in the organization of the University of Virginia, and that there was to be a President. In the circumstances there appeared to be unusual promise for a position like that of the University's Librarian.

So it was that in November 1902 Patton accepted appointment to the comparatively humble post of Assistant Librarian. It seems to have been understood, however, that there would be a change in the office of Librarian at the close of that session, 1902-1903. Actually there was a gap between the retirement of Librarian Page in June 1903 and the appointment of Patton as his successor in November of that year. But Patton had been named Acting Librarian for the interim; and when he did succeed to the position, it was at a salary, $1,150, that was greater than any one of the previous eight Librarians had received. As a gauge of the correctness of Patton's anticipations about the development of the position under the administration of the new President, it may be noted that the salary had reached $2,000 by 1914 and $3,000 by 1921, and that it was $3,600 during Patton's last session, 1926-1927.

2. PRESIDENT ALDERMAN

It can readily be seen that the years immediately following the Rotunda fire were strikingly different from the years which immediately preceded. That the first President of the University dates from 1904 is a manifestation of the change. The intensified administrative activities following 1895 made it increasingly evident that an organization with dual authority was placing heavy strain on both the Board of Visitors and the Faculty, and that some of the powers entrusted to each body could be performed more effectively if transferred to a single officer who would be in residence and who would not be engaged in instruction. This did not mean that either the Visitors or the Faculty had failed. The current Board of Visitors was a distinguished and a loyal body, and the Faculty had just given an unsurpassed demonstration of vigor and wise leadership. That each body was now willing to surrender some of its powers was not proof of insolvency, but rather of a notable spirit of courageous enterprise.

It was therefore under favorable auspices that Edwin Anderson Alderman became the first President of the University of Virginia. He had been a pioneer in educational expansion, first in North Carolina and then in the wider South. He had been President of the state-supported University of North Carolina, and President of Tulane

University, an institution largely supported by private endowments. The types of experience thus gained all reached fruition in the extremely active first years of his administration in Virginia. During those years the annual appropriation from the State was doubled. As the result of an intensive and exhausting campaign, an endowment fund of over a million dollars augmented the financial resources of the University. A "School" of Education was added to the university organization, followed by extension lectures; the University took over summer courses which since 1898 had been independently maintained as a School of Methods; and it was made evident that the University was prepared to cooperate fully in the educational programme of the State.

These advances were along the lines of President Alderman's earlier experiences. But the new spirit permeated all parts of the University; and there were many besides the President to whom credit should be given for the achievements of this period. Armistead Churchill Gordon, Rector from 1906 to 1918, handled with tact and wisdom the delicate matter of the adjustments of the Board of Visitors to the new form of administration. The Faculty, under the leadership of Dean James Morris Page, who had been the last Chairman of the Faculty, undertook the difficult task of standardizing the college and graduate school requirements, with such success that the University of Virginia became the first southeastern institution to be elected a member of the Association of American Universities. Graduate courses were separated from college courses, and a Department of Graduate Studies was organized in 1904 with Richard Heath Dabney as its first Dean. Visible signs of growth appeared in the form of an half dozen new buildings: Minor Hall for the Department of Law, Peabody Hall for the Department of Education, additions to the University Hospital, Madison Hall as a home for the Young

71

Men's Christian Association, and the President's house on Carr's Hill and the Commons, both erected from architectural designs prepared by Stanford White. There were improvements in the grounds and in the commercial buildings at "The Corner" and the Senff Gateway was erected at the main entrance to the University.

As for the changes in the organization of the University, the adjustments which followed the appointment of President Alderman form, in scope, in methods, and in effect, a highly instructive chapter in administration. For illustration we limit ourselves to what is pertinent to this historical sketch; namely, to the changes as they affected the University Library.

Those changes were in the direction of simplification. After 1906 no Library Committee of the Board of Visitors was appointed; and after that same date the Library Committee of the Faculty tended more and more to report directly to the President, who was *ex officio* a member of that committee, and not to the Faculty. The membership of the Faculty Library Committee was gradually increased until it came to be a body in size and also in function much like the Faculty of the earlier years. The Librarian acted as Secretary for the Faculty Library Committee, but he was not a voting member. In the preparation of the annual library budget and in the selection of a Librarian the Faculty Committee acted as an advisory body. The decisions rested with the President, though they were still subject to review and formal approval by the Rector and Visitors.

The new President quickly revealed an interest in the Library. In his early years as a Professor at the University of North Carolina he had been charged with the responsibility for the Library at that institution. He had then expressed his conviction that there should be an evolution of the College Library "from a mere array of books to a vital force in the educational life of the institution." This was an expression in general terms. In a talk to students at the University of Virginia on "books and reading" at one of the College Hours which he instituted, he made it clear that his primary concern was in the general cultural effect of a Library rather than in the support of college courses or, as yet at least, in research. In this respect his attitude would seem to have been not unlike Thomas Jefferson's—though President Alderman did not share the Founder's interest in library techniques.

At any rate, the Library benefited from the general university prosperity, just as it had in the 1850's—though at neither time was the Library a chief object of concern. There were moderate increases in the annual appropriations for the purchase of books, and the acquisition of books for general reading was encouraged. A first experiment, during 1907-1909, to add evening hours of opening did not attract sufficient readers to make its continuance appear practical. But a later attempt, in 1914, was more successful. In accord with the University's increased emphasis on statewide services to education, Librarian Patton joined with the Extension Division in introducing the circulation of package libraries among schools; and, in contrast to earlier attitudes, there was a definite tendency to liberalize loans from the Library. As we have seen, salary advances were indicative of increased appreciation of the importance of the position of Librarian. Moreover, after Patton's appointment, there was no reversion to a one person Library Staff. The position of Assistant Librarian was continued after 1903, the first regular appointee following Patton's brief tenure of that office being Anna Seeley Tuttle. Gradually other staff members were added, mainly in order to take care of the extended hours of opening and of the ever pressing problem of cataloguing. There was also a new field of activity opened by the introduction into the Summer Quarter in 1911 of a course in Library Methods,

73

given by Librarian Patton. In 1915 another course, taught by the then Assistant Librarian, Mary Louise Dinwiddie, was added, and such summer courses continued to be offered for many years.

In the courses on Library Methods there was consideration of the classification and cataloguing of books. We have observed in the previous history of the University of Virginia Library that the forward steps in the realization of librarianship as professional in character had for the most part been linked with emphasis on classification or cataloguing. That realization faintly emerged when in 1825 and 1828 Librarians Kean and Wertenbaker were in turn called upon to catalogue, i.e., to list, the books according to the Bacon-Jefferson classification. It came into the open in 1857 when Librarian Holcombe was enjoined to compile author and subject lists by a cataloguing method devised by Professor Gildersleeve and modified by the Board of Visitors. Holcombe completed an author list. Since no subject list was then or later achieved, it is not clear how far it would have followed the Bacon-Jefferson division of subjects. But by the shelving arrangements maintained during the terms of William Wertenbaker as Librarian, and followed by his pupil, Frederick Page, the Bacon-Jefferson system prevailed, at least in modified form, until the Rotunda fire. Shortly before the fire, two actions of significance were taken. One was the adoption of the card form in cataloguing. The other was the temporary employment of an "educated librarian" to begin a card catalogue, thus reversing the previous insistence that the work be done by the Librarian. In the confusion after the fire, the Bacon-Jefferson classification, like the old soldier in the General's ballad, seems not to have died, but just faded away. The same system's contemporary demise at the Library of Congress had been caused not by destruction of the books but quite otherwise—by the difficulty of applying its meagre and inelastic coverage of

74

the expanded fields of learning to a library collection grown to a million volumes. Out of expert study of those million volumes there came into being a new Library of Congress classification. This, however, was being quietly developed at that Library, with apparently little thought at first that it would be adopted for other collections. Meantime another system, the Dewey Decimal Classification, had become popularly known, particularly among public libraries, and it was this system that then came into use at the University of Virginia.

Thus began, under Librarian Patton and in connection with the second university collection, the most ambitious attempt at cataloguing that had yet been made. The magnitude of the task was still inadequately realized, and the first applications of the Dewey Decimal Classification were necessarily of the trial and error variety. Yet commendable progress was made by Miss Tuttle, by Katherine Crenshaw Ricks, who succeeded her for the session of 1911-1912, and by Mary Louise Dinwiddie, who was appointed an Assistant in 1911 and Assistant Librarian in 1912, and who continued in the latter office until her retirement in 1950, thereby achieving the Library's record to date for an unbroken term of service. A first attempt in this new cataloguing effort was to shelve the books in the order of their classification and to compile a shelf list—an arrangement, that is, of single card entries in the order of the books as shelved. This was a slow process; and to expedite matters it was decided to rearrange this shelf list as an author catalogue. The reward came in an increased use of the books, the annual records of circulation reaching totals never before attained.

Further specialization in the library routines developed from the increase in circulation and from the extension of the hours of opening. Lilie Estelle Dinwiddie, who had followed her sister by becoming an Assistant in 1912, from 1914 was placed in charge of circulation. By 1919, when she resigned to marry Professor Richard Lee Morton of the College of William and Mary, she had attractively demonstrated the value of emphasis on the quality of the circulation services. Later in this period, the Assistant Librarian, Mary Louise Dinwiddie, gave attention to starting more systematic procedures in the ordering of books and in the recording of periodicals.

An event notable for libraries had occurred in 1901 when the Library of Congress, under the inspiring leadership of Herbert Putnam, announced its willingness to distribute printed library cards. In 1909 the Faculty Library Committee approved the purchase and use of these at the University of Virginia. Previous to this, the Faculty as a whole had given an example of the cooperation that was later to be emphasized as a dominant policy of this Library, when it considered at length, in 1904, the making of an application for a depository set of the Library of Congress cards. The decision was that the influence of the University should be directed towards the location of a Virginia depository set at the State Library at Richmond.

It has been noted that a few weeks before the Rotunda fire, Librarian Page had prepared for the *Alumni Bulletin* a brief history of the University Library. This was one of several contributions by him of articles on the University. The role of the Librarian as author was emphasized by his successor. Throughout his administration Librarian Patton maintained a steady output of articles and books. In recognition he was appointed one of the Editors of the *Alumni Bulletin*. Beginning in 1913 he compiled a *Bulletin of the University of Virginia Library*. Until funds for printing failed in 1923, fourteen numbers of this Bulletin had been issued. There were also separate library publications, including a pamphlet on the Byrd collection and a small library handbook, both of which appeared in 1914.

The title of this little handbook, *The Library: An*

Invitation, is significant of the emphasis, during those active years, on President Alderman's conception of a library's services. Unfortunately, however, that rapid progress was not to be maintained. Two years prior to the appearance of the handbook, the health of the new President had been endangered by the strain of those first strenuous years, and late in 1912 he was forced to go to Saranac Lake, New York, for long months of treatment. It was the spring of 1914 before he was able to leave Saranac, and then it was for a leisurely trip with Mrs. Alderman to Switzerland. But that trip was fated not to be leisurely. Instead it ended in a hurried and adventurous departure from Europe in the midst of the confused beginning of the first world war.

3. GIFTS AND THE STATUS QUO

The coming of war vitally changed the situation at the University. The change was not as drastic as it had been during the War of 1861-1865, for Virginia was not in the region of the conflict. But attention was increasingly diverted from purely academic matters; and when in 1917 the United States entered actively on the side of the Allies, there were extensive enlistments by students and professors in the armed forces of the United States, and the reduced university community itself moved in the direction of becoming a military training post. As in the previous war, and as was again to happen in the second world war, the contributions in patriotic service comprised noble chapters in the University's history.

The reduction in student enrollment of course curtailed the income of the University; and as usual the Library proved to be a nerve center peculiarly sensitive to such curtailment. Appropriations were cut, the evening hours were discontinued, and there was a considerable decrease in the purchase of books and periodicals. Moreover, circumstances prolonged this library situation well beyond the war years by concentrating attention on other than library developments. The war had stimulated interest in scientific progress, especially in the fields of Chemistry and Medicine, and emphasis was naturally given to those subjects. Events connected with the centennial celebration of the establishment of the University and with a second endowment campaign absorbed general interest. The celebration was held, not in 1919, one hundred years after the granting of the charter, but in connection with the final exercises of the session of 1920-1921. Shortly afterwards there emerged a severely agitating legislative controversy over the possible removal of the Medical Department to Richmond. This was settled in a manner satisfactory to the University, but only after drawing all the forces of the University into an exhausting maelstrom of effort. During the war and postwar years the library services were steadily maintained, and accessions by gift continued to be received. But it was not until toward the close of the first hundred years, in 1925, that the Library's needs were pushed into the foreground.

The accessions by gift had, as we have seen, been extraordinarily numerous following the Rotunda disaster. The inflow continued without abatement after the coming of President Alderman. He was rarely gifted in understanding what objects would appeal to individual donors; and he was himself convinced that the Library was a worthy object. As those donations were a distinguishing feature of this whole period, we shall now supplement the illustrative list of the 1895-1904 donations by a similar list for the years 1904 to 1925. Since the dates of the gifts are given, it will be noted that the only break in the continuity was during the years of acute concentration on the war.

The donations of books included one in 1906 by Grace Dodge of New York City of approximately a thousand volumes appropriate for the students' reading room in the

78

newly opened Madison Hall. In 1907 the gift of books on Geology which had belonged to Jed Hotchkiss, the Virginia geologist and topographer, led to the establishment of a separate Geology Library in the Brooks Museum. This donation came from his widow. Later the same year the University received word of the bequest by Edward Wilson James of Norfolk of his private library of some 12,000 volumes. The following year, 1908, the Law Library was the recipient of a long run of the Reports of the English Courts from Dean James Barr Ames of the Harvard Law School. In 1910, the French Government, through Ambassador Jusserand, presented a valuable set of works of the art, history, and literature of France. By bequest of Judge Lambert Tree of Chicago in 1911 the Law Library became the possessor of his law books. To the Medical Library in 1912 came a donation of books and journals on Pediatrics from William David Booker of Baltimore. In 1913 there was an especially rich harvest. This included books from the estate of Professor Harrison which met immediate needs of curriculum courses and which supplemented the collection on Southern authors which Professor Harrison had been instrumental in starting. It also included the choice library of Bennett Wood Green, who had been a resident of the University at the time of his death, and whose affection for his books gave them associative value to those who had had the good fortune of knowing him. That year's harvest likewise included the first consignment of the private collection of Wilbur Phelps Morgan, a physician of Baltimore and a bookman of catholic tastes. The Morgan donations continued until his death in 1922, and reached a total of well over 10,000 volumes. In 1915 came another gift of both intrinsic and association values, in the books of Andrew Stevenson, presented by his granddaughter. Andrew Stevenson had been a member of the Board of Visitors from 1845 to 1857 and its Rector from 1856 to

1857. Prior to those dates he had been a member and the Speaker of the Virginia House of Delegates, a member and the Speaker of the House of Representatives in Washington, and Minister to England.

The tide of donations again reached the flood stage after the first world war. In 1920 the working library of William Harry Heck, Professor of Education from 1905 until his death in 1919, was presented by his widow, Anna Tuttle Heck, who had been Assistant Librarian from 1903 to 1911. This led to the establishment in Peabody Hall of the Heck Memorial Library in Education. Early in the following year, 1921, the eminent international lawyer, John Bassett Moore, announced his intention of presenting to the Law Library his extensive collection of works on international law. Portions continued to be received until after his death in 1947, giving distinction to the University's holdings in that subject. In 1922 there were received approximately 8,000 volumes from the private library of William Gordon McCabe, educator and author of international reputation. These volumes were presented by William Gordon McCabe, Jr., as a memorial to his father and to his elder brother. The father had been an officer in the Confederate Army, the founder and head of the University School, located at first at Petersburgh and later at Richmond, and a member of the University of Virginia Board of Visitors from 1887 to 1896. His wide acquaintance included such English writers as Matthew Arnold, Browning, and Tennyson. In that same year, 1922, the Law Library received from Judge George Moffett Harrison of Staunton, Virginia, approximately 600 volumes from his private library; and the following year there was another notable donation to the Law Library, this coming from Judge Legh Richmond Watts of Portsmouth, Virginia, and consisting of some 1,400 volumes. In 1924 there came to the Chemistry Library over 1,000 books bequeathed by Charles Baskerville, a graduate of the University of Virginia who had been Professor of Chemistry at the College of the City of New York from 1904 until his death in 1924.

As yet there had been no systematic organization of a rare book collection. Some rare items had been recognized among the gifts and isolated for special protection. Several rarities had been received as individual gifts. Such were three items given in 1913 by Mrs. Martha Jefferson Trist Burke of Alexandria, Virginia: a Bible which had been presented by George Wythe to Thomas Jefferson, and the two copies of the New Testament from which Jefferson had clipped the portions used by him in preparing his compilation known as *The Life and Morals of Jesus of Nazareth.* Other Jefferson items were a copy of the first American edition of the *Notes on the State of Virginia,* given by Frank Pierce Brent of Christchurch, Virginia; and a copy of Wythe's *Virginia Reports,* published in 1795, a copy annotated both by George Wythe and by Thomas Jefferson, which was presented by Jefferson Randolph Kean, a grandson of John Vaughan Kean, the first Librarian, and, on his mother's side, a great grandson of Jefferson.

For the Lee Papers and other manuscripts a special case had been procured in 1913, and a number of pieces, chiefly Jefferson letters, were added to the manuscript collection during the years 1895 to 1925. Among the donors of manuscripts were Mrs. Francis Eppes Shine of Los Angeles, California, Mrs. Mary Madison McGuire of Washington, D.C., and William Andrews Clark, Jr., also of Los Angeles and of Butte, Montana. Several years after the Rotunda fire there was discovered a cache of papers which had apparently been rescued on that October Sunday, tucked away for safety, and then forgotten. There was a lighter side to this treasure trove. Among the papers unearthed was a library fine list for the second session in which was entered a charge of sixty cents against Edgar Allan Poe for the late return

81

of a book, followed by a notation that fifty-eight cents had been paid. This was of course grist for the news mill. Not long after, a communication was received from the girl students of the American Literature class of Virginia Intermont College at Bristol in far southwest Virginia, enclosing a two cent stamp to clear the poet's record!

An acquisition of source material on Poe, along with a gratifying illustration of the cooperative spirit, came in 1921 through the efforts of Dr. James Southall Wilson, who had in 1919 been appointed Edgar Allan Poe Professor of English. The biographer John H. Ingram, an English champion of Poe, had for over forty years been collecting personal letters, pictures, rare editions, and miscellaneous items concerning the poet's life. After Ingram's death in 1916, his sister Laura had offered to sell the bulk of the collection (disposition had already been made of some of the choice pieces) to the University of Virginia. Librarian Patton had proposed that the material be shipped from England to Charlottesville for examination, the transportation charges to be paid by the University. However, the dangers from German submarines during World War I had made such transfer seem unwise, and further consideration of the matter had lapsed. When the shipping lanes again became safe, Miss Ingram passed on the offer of purchase to the University of Texas. The response, written by Professor Killis Campbell, had been that the University of Texas would be interested, but that it would first wish to have assurance that the University of Virginia had refused. It was at this moment that Professor Wilson learned of the situation. He persuaded President Alderman and the Faculty Library Committee to draw from certain accumulated funds, and the negotiations were successfully completed. A real beginning of an important research collection on Poe was thus achieved.

An unusual feature of the gifts during those years was

the donation by several authors of remainder stocks from their works, with the privilege of profit to the Library by sales. The works included the *Word-Book of Virginia Folk-Speech* by Bennett Wood Green, the five volumes of the quaint *Lower Norfolk County Antiquary,* edited and in large part written by Edward Wilson James, and *A Reprint of Annual Reports and Other Papers on the Geology of the Virginias* by William Barton Rogers.

There was also a notable increase in library endowment funds during the years of the Alderman administration to 1925, amounting to a principal of approximately $200,000. About five-eights of this came in 1913 from the estate of Bennett Wood Green. The other endowment funds were established chronologically as follows: in 1909 the William Whitehead Fuller Fund for the Law Library; in 1911 the William Barton Rogers Fund for the Physics Library and the Lambert Tree Fund for the General Library; in 1919 the Ferrell Dabney Minor, Jr., Memorial Fund for the Law Library and the Isabel Mercein Tunstall Fund for books of poetry for the General Library; in 1920 the James Douglas Bruce Fund for English Literature, this being chiefly used for the Graduate Library; in 1922 the Walter H. Jones Fund for journals for the Engineering Library and the Coolidge Fund, established for the Law Library in memory of Thomas Jefferson by the Coolidge Family of Boston; and in 1923 the Hamilton M. Barksdale Funds for the Chemistry and Engineering Libraries. In addition several thousand dollars were donated for immediate expenditure. These gifts included one from Robert Baylor Tunstall, Sr., in 1907 to establish the Isabel Mercein Tunstall Collection of Poetry, for which, as stated above, an endowment fund was later presented, one from Arthur Curtiss James in 1912 for books on the Negro, one from Paul Goodloe McIntire in 1919 for books and equipment for the School of Fine Arts, one from Alfred William

83

Erickson in 1922 for the Education Library, and two in 1923, the first contributed by an anonymous donor for the General Library, and the second raised by the members of Minor Inn of Phi Delta Phi for the purchase of law books in memory of Raleigh Colston Minor.

This was a truly remarkable outpouring of gifts; and the Library's growth in size of collection maintained the pace set in the first years after the Rotunda fire. It will be recalled that on the afternoon of the disastrous day there had remained 17,194 volumes as a nucleus for a new library collection. It was a small nucleus for an institution seventy years in being. But by June 1925, thirty years later, the reported figure was 131,422, an increase of over sevenfold. That was the reported figure. There doubtless were by that time more books in the possession of the University. But both lack of Staff and lack of shelf space were preventing full use of the library resources. Given books as well as purchased books require technical handling to render them accessible. As early as 1914 Librarian Patton was making an urgent plea for a larger Library Staff in order that the accumulated work behind the scenes might be accomplished. Between then and 1925 the situation at the Rotunda steadily increased in complexity and confusion. A natural result may readily be seen in the very listing of the gifts. For a large proportion of the gifts were for separate libraries. It was at least in part because of administrative difficulties that the University Library became the University Libraries.

The dispersion had started before 1895, when already the inadequacy of the Rotunda was becoming recognized. At that date there were four Libraries. There were also a Mathematics Reading Room and reading rooms for students and for professors. By 1925 the number of special collections had grown to thirteen. The nine new ones were the Classical Library in Cabell Hall, the Education Library in Peabody Hall, the Engineering Library in the Mechanical Laboratory, the Geology Library in the Brooks Museum, the Graduate Library in the pavilion on West Lawn used as an office for the Department of Graduate Studies, the Mathematics Library in Cabell Hall, the Medical Library in one of the oval rooms on the first floor of the Rotunda which had been vacated by the Law Library when the latter was moved to Minor Hall, the Physics Library in the Rouss Physical Laboratory, and the Y.M.C.A. Library in Madison Hall. All of these locations except that for the Medical Library were outside of the Rotunda; and all these libraries, including the Medical, were, to some degree at least, independent organizations.

A word should be inserted about the collections which, being outside of the Rotunda on 27 October 1895, had not suffered from the fire. For one of them, the Chemistry Library, that good fortune did not continue. For it was totally destroyed in 1917 by the burning of the Chemical Laboratory. A vigorous start was at once made on another collection; and this was located in 1918 in the new Cobb Chemical Laboratory. In this case, the availability of the Barksdale Chemistry Fund after 1923 helped to make a plan for systematic coverage of the subject possible, the carrying out of the plan being entrusted to Professor John Howe Yoe. The manna of special funds did not fall on the Astronomy or Biology Libraries. But the annual effort to solicit gifts and exchanges was patiently maintained by the Faculty of the School of Astronomy; and an effort by Miss Dinwiddie to catalogue the Biology collection was of assistance towards the use of that Library.

Two of the three reading rooms were among the sufferers at the time of the Rotunda fire. The mathematics reading room had been in the Annex and the students' reading room in the wing connecting the Rotunda with West Lawn. Both of these made fresh starts as separate library collections, and have been included in the list of nine separate libraries, the Madison Hall Library continuing the students' reading room. The faculty reading room seems to have died a natural death. But the present-day display of periodicals in the Colonnade Club may be a reincarnation.

As for the Law Library, its record had been one of notable good fortune. It is true that it was to the fated Annex that its books were removed from the gallery of the main library just prior to the fire. But that room in the Annex was easily accessible, and from it the books, including a number from Jefferson's original list, were salvaged in the early minutes of the conflagration. Moreover in the receipt of gifts of books and funds, it had been specially favored. Its needs had also been given some recognition in most of the annual budgets. Faculty awareness of its value for legal training had led to careful planning for library space and equipment in the new law building, Minor Hall. To that building the Law Library was moved in 1911. Beginning in 1896 student Law Librarians had annually been appointed. In 1911 the position was made full time, with Ella Watson Johnson as the first appointee. She was followed in 1912 by Catherine Rebecca Lipop, who continued as Law Librarian until her retirement in 1945, the only change being one of name, since in 1925 she became Mrs. Charles Alfred Graves—thus following Mrs. Anna Tuttle Heck in acquiring faculty status not as a Librarian but by marriage! By 1925 the Law Library contained more than 20,000 volumes, and was by far the largest of the separate collections.

The new home of the Law Library in Minor Hall was to prove reasonably adequate for the next two decades. The restored Rotunda, however, created growing pains for the General Library almost from the start. Early in President Alderman's administration something had been done towards improving the attractiveness and the comfort of the library room. But Librarian Patton was soon adding lack of shelf space to lack of Staff in his enumeration of his administrative difficulties. The early expressions were cautious and somewhat vague. But by 1917 it was stated in his annual report that "The truth is, the Rotunda is already inadequate for the whole library, and another building, planned and made to provide stackrooms, reading rooms, office and other facilities necessary to modern library development and administration is already a pressing need —a need which touches more students than any other." This wording still did not suggest more than a college library; and the plea, however justified, gained merely a sympathetic hearing. But with the appointment of John Calvin Metcalf as Chairman of the Faculty Library Committee in 1918 and as Dean of the Department of Graduate Studies in 1923, the cause of the Library was reinforced by its relation to the University's responsibility for the means of research. The new concept involved much more than a building. But the building was the first essential.

Two events which occurred at this stage were revealing. In the plans for the programme of the Centennial Celebration there was included a banquet in the Rotunda for the guests and participants. It will be recalled that in 1824, before the Rotunda had been completed and before the University had actually opened, there had been held in that building a community banquet to Lafayette. It will be recalled also that there had later been objection to the use of the library room for other than library purposes—in particular for dancing. There were therefore precedents both for the action by John Lloyd Newcomb, Dean of the Department of Engineering and the able General Chairman of the Centennial Committee, in designating the Rotunda as the place of this banquet; and for the action by Dean Metcalf, Chairman of the Faculty Library Committee, in warning of the damage that might result from such use of the crowded library room. Here were two emergencies meeting head on. The result was a compromise. It was decided that the banquet should be held in the Rotunda, and that the Centennial Committee should help out the library situation by donating the cost of three bookcases. This was admitted to be merely a temporary solution. Later these two officers were to be leaders in the ultimate effort to secure a new library building.

The three bookcases barely alleviated the Library's shelving problem, and the second event was a further effort to add to the book capacity of the Rotunda. The northeast wing had been secured in 1914 for the housing of government documents, and efforts were started towards having history classes transferred from the northwest wing in order to free it for use as a periodical stack and reading room. Plans prepared by the Assistant Librarian, Miss Dinwiddie, for a rearrangement of the equipment in the circular library room were approved in 1921, and shelving was purchased for the second gallery. In order to finance these latter changes, the Faculty Library Committee was compelled to take the drastic action of drawing from funds allocated for the purchase of books. The added endowments had increased the annual income. Nevertheless this equipment expenditure had to be carried for several years as an overdraft, with sharp limitation of book purchases and periodical subscriptions. By January 1924 the Faculty Library Committee, in discussing what had come to be a perennial plea for small appropriations for equipment, decided to call a halt to this piecemeal procedure and to throw its whole weight behind the new building project. Its statement, prepared by Chairman Metcalf for presentation to President Alderman and, through him, to the Board of Visitors, was the most definite and powerful that had yet been made. It still had to be met with the response that no funds were available. But the cogency and force of the argument were not without effect. Three months later, in his 1924 Founder's Day address, President Alderman, in a summary beginning, "And now may I dream a few dreams," outlined his considered hopes for future development of the University. Eight objects were specified, of which the first was an endowment for research, and the third "a great new library, costing a million dollars."

The first hundred years of the University Library thus ended. The burning of the Rotunda had sharply interrupted continuity of the century's progress. That disaster had well-nigh destroyed the library collection which had been so nobly started by Thomas Jefferson. The thirty years which followed brought the encouragement of the rapid growth of a new collection, obtained mainly from generous gifts. They brought also the discouragement of crowded, scattered, and unworkable conditions. There seemed to be a stalement. But there were also the beginnings of a new and more adequate conception of a University Library.

V

The Librarians
of the First Hundred Years

THERE WERE nine Librarians during the first hundred years of the University of Virginia Library. In the preceding historical sketch there have been recorded details concerning the library services of each of the nine, with some indication of the place of each in the slowly changing conception of the position of Librarian. But Librarians are persons; and it now seems fitting to throw such light as may be possible on the backgrounds and personal characteristics of those nine. An effort will be made to keep repetition at a minimum. Therefore, to complete each picture, what has already been noted in the historical sketch should be added to the personal records which follow. In some cases the outlines will still be faint. It would seem that Librarians not infrequently qualify for the role of the unknown citizen.

These were nine quite different personalities, and one cannot from them generalize about the attitude of the community toward the genus Librarian. But the comment of one shrewd observer, David Culbreth, who was a student at the University midway in those hundred years, from 1872 to 1877, is suggestive. He was writing of the one of the nine, William Wertenbaker, whose librarianship covered nearly half, forty-three years, of the century. "While the students," said Culbreth in his book, *The University of Virginia: Memories of Her Student-Life and Professors,* "never placed him on the same plane with the professors, yet they appeared to look upon him as a kind of paternal spirit deserving all honor and kindness."

1. JOHN VAUGHAN KEAN (1803-1876)
LIBRARIAN 1825

The first Librarian, John Vaughan Kean, had the shortest term, one year. It will be recalled that during 1825 the collection of books was small, it was temporarily located in a pavilion on West Lawn, and it was open for students only one hour a week. The salary was $150 for the session. Yet there were a number of applications for the position. The one received from Dr. Andrew Kean in behalf of his son found favor, probably because of Jefferson's high regard for the father. Doctor Kean's home was in Goochland County, but his reputation had extended throughout central Virginia. It was said that, when the dates for his visits to distant cases became known, patients would be brought to the roadside to await his passing. At any rate, Jefferson and others had urged this "beloved old Doctor" to take up his residence in Charlottesville; and there is reliable testimony that Andrew Kean was offered the chair of Medicine at the new University. But he seems to have felt himself to be better qualified for general practice than for teaching.

It was the son who was to be the teacher. John Vaughan Kean had been born in 1803, and, according to his father's letter of application to Rector Jefferson, possessed "a good English education, a tolerable acquaintance with the Latin and some slight knowledge of the Greek languages." These had been acquired before he enrolled as a student in the University of Virginia. At the University his courses for that first session were in the "Schools" of Chemistry, Mathematics, Modern Languages, and Natural Philosophy. These courses and the enforcement of the library regulations under the supervision of Rector Jefferson and the Faculty doubtless gave young Kean a busy year. Meantime his father, after a short stay in Charlottesville, had decided to return to his home and practice in Goochland County; and at the end of the session the son resigned from the University and from the library post and started a school at Olney in Caroline County, Virginia. He was thus one of the first of a distinguished company of secondary school administrators and teachers who had the prestige of training at the University of Virginia. At Olney he married, raised a family of considerable size, became "Schoolmaster Napoleon Kean with the little head of all knowledge," and lived until 1876. One of his pupils later described his manner as *suaviter in modo, fortiter in re*. As a phrase, this pleasantly demonstrated the classical training received at the Olney School. As a description, it may well be that there is here a trace of the effect on the impressionable student-librarian of a year's association with Thomas Jefferson.

That librarianship was brief, but Kean's later links with the University and its Library through his family have been close. A son of his, Robert Garlick Hill Kean, was a student at the University, became a leading lawyer of Lynchburg, Virginia, a member of the Board of Visitors of the University from 1872 to 1875 and again from 1890 to 1894, and the Rector of the Board from 1872 to 1875. This son married Jane Nicholas Randolph of Edgehill and thus became allied with the Randolph and Jefferson families. Their son, Jefferson Randolph Kean, was a graduate of the University's Department of Medicine, had a distinguished career in the Surgeon General's Department of the United States Army, and was instrumental in support of Walter Reed's achievements in the control of yellow fever. Toward the close of his life, General Kean joined with his son, Robert Hill Kean of Richmond, a doctor of philosophy of the University of Virginia, in making available at the

University Library papers and books of rare associative interest, since they had belonged to direct descendants of both the Founder of the University and of the University's first Librarian.

2. WILLIAM WERTENBAKER (1797-1882)
LIBRARIAN 1826-1831, 1835-1857, 1865-1881
LIBRARIAN EMERITUS 1881-1882

By contrast, the second Librarian, William Wertenbaker, holds the record for length of service. He was a native of Albemarle County, was present at the birth of the University of Virginia, and was a part of its life until he died at the age of eighty-five. He came of German stock which had migrated to Maryland about 1740. Sometime between 1783 and 1790 his father, Christian Wertenbaker, had moved to Virginia and settled at Milton in Albemarle County, his lot being next to one owned by Thomas Jefferson. It was there that William was born 1 June 1797. Later his mother, who had been Mary Grady of Caroline County, Virginia, inherited a farm northwest of Charlottesville, and the family moved thither. The farm was on the Old Barracks Road, so-called because it led to the encampment where in 1779 had been settled prisoners taken in the Revolutionary War. That location probably gave rise to the erroneous tradition that Christian Wertenbaker had been one of the Hessian soldiers.

While a boy of fourteen, William Wertenbaker obtained employment in the Clerk's Office in Charlottesville, Alexander Garrett then being Deputy Clerk. Only a year or two later, when a local company of militia was organized for service in the War of 1812, young Wertenbaker enlisted. The company was assigned to the brigade, under command of John Hartwell Cocke, which operated in eastern Virginia,

93

to protect the approaches to Richmond. Shortly after being mustered out, Wertenbaker, who had returned to his position in the Clerk's Office, was appointed Deputy Sheriff of Albemarle County. He also began the study of law in the office of Valentine Wood Southall, one of Charlottesville's leading lawyers; and it was with the intention of becoming a lawyer that Wertenbaker enrolled as a student at the opening of the University.

It is noteworthy that those early occupations of his attached this young man to persons intimately connected with the beginnings of the University of Virginia. General Cocke was one of the Founders of the University, and he was for thirty-three years an extraordinarily valuable member of its Board of Visitors. Alexander Garrett was a Trustee of Albemarle Academy, a member of the Board of Visitors of Central College, the Proctor of Central College, and the University's first Bursar. Valentine Wood Southall presided at the banquet held in the Rotunda in 1824 in honor of Lafayette. When on 6 October 1817 the cornerstone was laid of the pavilion that was to give visible form to Central College, it was Southall who delivered the address to the general audience and it was Garrett who, as Worthy Grand Master, officiated in the Masonic ritual. Moreover, on the contract for the erection of that pavilion there were the signatures of Alexander Garrett as Proctor of Central College, of William Wertenbaker as witness, and of Thomas Jefferson as endorsing approval in behalf of the Central College Board of Visitors.

It is altogether likely, therefore, that Rector Jefferson had some previous acquaintance with this student of the University's first session; and when Librarian Kean resigned, it seems not improbable that Jefferson chose Wertenbaker as Kean's successor because of his knowledge of the young man's previous experience with civic records, military discipline, and law enforcement. There is apparently no record that Wertenbaker had made application for the position.

It was Wertenbaker, therefore, who moved the library books into the Rotunda and was the first to put into operation in that building the regulations for library use. It was he, also, who performed the clerical task of compiling the 1828 printed catalogue. He continued as a student during the second session, a part of his courses being under John Tayloe Lomax, Professor of Law, who had joined the Faculty with that session. But Librarian Wertenbaker then had to interrupt his college work, and his intention of becoming a lawyer had eventually to be abandoned. For in 1829 he married Louisiana Timberlake, a sister of the wife of Warner Minor, one of the University's "Hotel-Keepers," and there ensued the responsibilities of a growing family. As his hours as Librarian were still few, Wertenbaker began to take on other income producing occupations, until he had, at one time or another, filled nearly all the positions available at the University except a Professor's chair. His collection at this time included Assistant Proctor, University Postmaster, and Bookstore Manager. Coincident with undertaking as a student the post of Librarian, he had also been appointed Secretary of the Faculty. There was at first some faculty objection at having (to quote Robert Burns) "a student chield amang them taking notes" of the very frank discussions in those early faculty meetings. But Wertenbaker's serious mien seems soon to have allayed apprehension on that score. In fact his demeanor could be so stern that there were reactions to his disadvantage. By performing the duties of Assistant Proctor with the methods of a former Deputy Sheriff, he aroused violent opposition on the part of spirited students who were approximately of his own age. There were incidents of violent language and of attacks directed at him, and one student was expelled in 1831 for repeated threats to flog Wertenbaker.

The Wertenbaker career as Librarian was interrupted for two periods, and the first interruption came at this time, in 1831. It has been conjectured that he wished to resume legal studies. But he did not register again as a student; and it is possible that there was some loss of confidence in him on the part of faculty members inclined to find reason in the student complaints. This is merely a guess. But he did at this time resign also as Secretary of the Faculty, and he ceased to be Assistant Proctor. He seems, however, to have continued as the local Postmaster and as Manager of the bookstore.

However, after four years of notoriously lax conduct of the Library by William Henry Brockenbrough, the Faculty and Visitors were quite ready to have Wertenbaker reappointed. During his next and longest term as Librarian, from 1835 to 1857, he added for one year, 1854-1855, the post of University Hotel Keeper to his collection of stipend producing activities. In all this he was meeting household expenses, not serving Mammon; and he freely devoted his efforts to causes which brought no monetary returns. For many years he was an active and respected member of the Session of the Charlottesville Presbyterian Church; and he was a leader, along with John Hartwell Cocke, his Commanding General in the War of 1812, in the early temperance movements at the University of Virginia.

In a preceding section of the historical sketch we have seen that the second interruption to Wertenbaker's career as Librarian came in 1857 as the result of the decision of the Board of Visitors to separate the library post from any other position. Wertenbaker continued to be Secretary of the Faculty through the war years and on until his retirement because of illness in 1881. As he held that secretaryship from 1826 to 1831 and from 1836 to 1881, a total of fifty years, and as he was also Secretary of the Board of Visitors for six years, 1865 to 1871, this scribe, who made no claim to devotion to literary pursuits, probably has to his credit more pages in his handwriting than any other contributor to the University Archives.

A veteran of the War of 1812-1814, he was too old for active service in the War of 1861-1865. But there was no question of his convictions. A memorable gathering at his house in March 1861, the month before the firing on Fort Sumter, was one of the early occasions of the raising of a Confederate flag. Of his three sons, the eldest, his namesake, had been killed as a boy by being thrown from a horse. The others, Charles Christian and Thomas Grady, had both been students in the University of Virginia, and both were officers in the Confederate Army. Thomas, who was one of the student organizers of the Young Men's Christian Association at the University of Virginia in 1858 and was studying for the Presbyterian ministry, lost his life in the war. Charles Christian survived and became a manufacturer in postwar Charlottesville. To a distinguished son of his, Professor Thomas Jefferson Wertenbaker of Princeton and Oxford Universities, acknowledgment is gladly made for friendly assistance in supplying some of the details here given concerning his grandfather, the Librarian.

Librarian Wertenbaker's last "tour of duty" at the Rotunda was from 1865 to 1881. He zealously continued his guardianship of the books. It was in this period that he made his vigorous protests against the holding of dances in the library room. By this time he had come to be the sole survivor of the original group of professors and administrative officers; and when illness made it impossible for him to continue the daily trips to the Library, the Board of Visitors took the unusual but heartily approved action of naming him Librarian Emeritus and of continuing his salary, then $700 a year, as long as he should live. But this new title he held for only one year, for his death came on 7 April 1882.

At the close of his long service, the estimated size of the

library collection was 36,000 volumes. This was between four and five times the 8,000 of 1830, but it was essentially an expansion of the nucleus originally selected by Jefferson. Wertenbaker was spared the knowledge that the nucleus and the additions were thirteen years later to be in large part destroyed by fire; and that his own agency in adding to the original collection was fated to have little effect on the new University Library collection that was to date from 1895.

Wertenbaker's agency in collection building was mainly in the purchase of the books, not in their selection, which had continued to be a faculty function. There was a pleasant exception, however. In the poverty-stricken period after the war, in November 1868 to be exact, a visitor from New York, Abiel Abbot Low, was so impressed by the Library and by its custodian's courteous demeanor, that, on leaving, he handed to Wertenbaker a cheque for five hundred dollars. The surprised Librarian inquired how the donor desired this money to be spent. "Do with it as you please," said Mr. Low. "I leave it entirely to your discretion." "My first love is the library," was Wertenbaker's prompt response. He immediately reported the gift to the Faculty, with the modestly offered recommendation that the money be used for "such standard works, of permanent value, on History & Biography, Geography & Travels, Religion and General Literature as may be of common interest to all the Professors and especially useful to the students of the University." The formal, comprehensive, and precise nature of the statement excellently reveals Wertenbaker's characteristic manner and motives. Maybe it is also a reminder of his absorption of Jefferson dicta concerning books and a library.

There is ample indication that during his terms as Librarian, Wertenbaker impressed students, faculty, and visitors not only as a disciplinarian but also, as University

Historian Bruce expressed it, by his "conspicuous fidelity, integrity, and efficiency." From his portrait, with a beard, by John Adams Elder and from a Bohn album engraving, without a beard, by A. B. Walter, and from word pictures by university graduates writing of their student days, an attempt at a composite delineation of William Wertenbaker is possible. The writers of reminiscences were Paul Brandon Barringer and Francis Henry Smith, who became Professors at the University of Virginia; David Marvel Reynolds Culbreth, physician of Baltimore; Richard McIlwaine, Presbyterian clergyman and President of Hampden-Sydney College; and Crawford Howell Toy, Professor of Hebrew at Harvard University.

This delineation is of his later years. He was of medium height—about five feet, eight inches—and he weighed approximately one hundred and forty-five pounds. He walked with a cane, leaning slightly forward, and his gait was deliberate. His face was small, with a high forehead, strong features, a long upper lip, and a firm mouth. He was commonly addressed as "Mr. Wert"—but student references to him were likely to be to "Old Wert." His usual greeting to students, whatever the time of day, was "Good morning." For, he would explain, "These young men are in the morning of life." In general his manner was reserved, never familiar or obtrusive, friendly, but strictly businesslike. By interested and appreciative listeners he could be induced to expand into stories of the early days of the University, of his conversations with Jefferson and Madison and the other Founders, and of his impressions of the early Professors—of the time, for example, when at a faculty meeting the Professor of Mathematics kicked the Professor of Modern Languages under the table, and the latter retorted: "You kick like an ass." He was an early defender of Poe against his detractors. He had a retentive and accurate memory; it enabled him readily to locate books

99

on the shelves, to know the names of the students and to be able to enumerate what books each had borrowed, and to greet graduates by name when they returned to visit the University. He seemed never to be idle. For relaxation from his varied duties, he would settle down comfortably to a game of chess.

There were, it is true, some derogatory comments on the management of the Library during those days. As one critic stated it—it may be noted that he was anonymous—"The Library was not the heart of the University." He pointed out that students were "allowed" the use of the Library, that stiff regulations were strictly enforced, and that the hours of opening were not liberal. In part, however, this condition was not so much the result of the administration of the Library as it was of the methods of instruction. The methods were those of lectures and textbook recitations, not of collateral and reference readings from books reserved in the Library. The close cooperation of the Library with the curriculum came much later. Indeed it was years after Wertenbaker's time that, according to an unauthenticated tale, one faculty member's objection to evening hours of opening was, forsooth, that the students might be tempted to read books when they should be studying their lessons!

Yet some of those very criticisms of the Library in Wertenbaker's day are capable of another interpretation. His greatest treasure, which he would display as a climax to an especially friendly conversation, was Jefferson's letter to him of 30 January 1826. There, in the well-known handwriting, were these words:

An important part of your charge will be to keep the books in a state of sound preservation, undefaced, and free from injury by moisture or other accident, and in their stated arrangement on the shelves according to the method and order of their catalogue. your other general duties and rules of conduct are prescribed in the printed collection of the enactments of the Board of Visitors. of these rules the Board will expect the strictest observance on your own part, and that you use the utmost care and vigilance that they be strictly observed by others.

We have seen that this letter grew out of an emergency action by Jefferson, the appointment of a student as custodian of the books in order to maintain the operation of the Library, and that it does not necessarily limit the Founder's conception of the functions of librarianship. But from 1826 to Wertenbaker's last active hours in 1881, those were his marching orders from Thomas Jefferson; and whatever else might happen, those orders were to be obeyed. He had been entrusted with the Library by Mr. Jefferson, and he spent his manhood years in being faithful to that trust.

3. WILLIAM HENRY BROCKENBROUGH
(1812-1850)
LIBRARIAN 1831-1835

William Wertenbaker's first love was the Library. For William Henry Brockenbrough, who held the position from 1831 to 1835, the librarianship was a somewhat inconvenient means to other ends. The outcome with simple directness points a moral. Of the nine Librarians of this first hundred years, Brockenbrough was the one definite failure.

That failure was deserved. Brockenbrough drew the salary of the position, which was then $250 a year, but shirked its duties. It is fair, however, to add that the pressure of circumstances to which he yielded was strong. His family's fortunes were in eclipse, it was important that he obtain a law degree, and he seems to have been suffering from the early stages of tuberculosis.

His father, Arthur Spicer Brockenbrough, had been an

important factor in the building of the University. As Superintendent of Repairs at the State Capitol in Richmond, he had come to the attention of the Governor, James Patton Preston, and Governor Preston had recommended him for the post of Proctor of the University. There his energy, his common sense, and his constructive ideas appealed to Jefferson; and his intelligent comprehension of the Founder's plans and his constant presence at the point of operation rendered him an agent of marked value during the building period. In those days Charlottesville was an isolated town lacking transportation facilities, and there were no experienced contractors capable of translating specifications into reliable estimates of cost. To a large degree it was necessary for the Proctor to take on himself the gathering of materials and the training and superintendence of the workmen. These things Brockenbrough did to Jefferson's satisfaction—and Jefferson was a firm and observant principal for any such operations.

The importance of his position and the regard shown by Jefferson gave prestige to Arthur Brockenbrough during the first years. Socially he was linked with an early romance at the University, the wooing and wedding of Harriet Selden, his wife's sister, by George Long, the young Professor of Ancient Languages from the University of Cambridge. But along with his finer qualities, Brockenbrough was inclined to be impatient of ineptitude, whether in workmen or in members of the Faculty, and he had a quick temper. When the major construction tasks had been completed, and the Proctor's duties fell more into a routine of small jobs, his popularity waned; and in 1831 he was eased out of his position—though he was permitted to retain the title of Patron. His death followed not long after.

His son, William Henry Brockenbrough, had become a student of the University in 1828 and was pressing assiduously towards a law degree. His father's loss of position and income greatly handicapped that effort. It seems possible that his appointment in 1831 as Librarian (he was a student, as Kean and Wertenbaker had been at the time of their appointments) was influenced by sympathy for his situation on the part of some of the Visitors and Faculty.

The appointment came in July, to take effect in August. Almost at once his attitude and the criticism thereat became apparent. His effort to continue as candidate for a degree without further registration or payment of fees drew from the Faculty an action specifically aimed at him in February 1832 and again in October of that year. In July 1833 the Board of Visitors granted an application for a room in a vacant hotel but seems to have taken no action on his claim for compensation for certain temporary shops erected on university grounds by his father. As late as August 1834 a letter of his to Joseph C. Cabell of the Board of Visitors indicates that he was still involved in certain matters connected with his father's proctorship.

As for his management of the Library, adverse criticism began early and grew in volume. The Visitors' Library Committee, whose function at first, it will be recalled, was chiefly to make an annual inspection, reported in July 1832, after one year of Brockenbrough's tenure of the librarianship, that there was need of a house cleaning of the Rotunda and there should be stricter enforcement of the library regulations. A somewhat similar report was made by the Visitors' Committee in July 1833. By October 1834 a special committee of the Faculty, headed by Professor Emmet, had been appointed by that body to examine into the state of the Library. A month later this Committee presented an elaborate report, charging the Librarian with the down-at-the-heel condition of the equipment, with lack of orderly arrangement of the books, with laxity in enforcement of the regulations, with frequent absences without previous notice, and with appointment of assistants who had not been approved by the Faculty. In the discovery ten years after the opening of the Library that the equipment was deteriorating and that some of the regulations needed clarification, it would seem that the Faculty had its share in any possible blame; and in view of the antagonism that had been developing between Faculty and students in this decade, it was not unnatural that a student appointee should join in the student attitude toward what appeared to be illiberal rules. But for his lack of responsibility as a custodian of the books there was no excuse.

The long report was presented to the Faculty on 11 November 1834. It was a bad break for Librarian Brockenbrough that the following week a severe rainstorm descended on Charlottesville, sundry leaks in the Rotunda began active operation, and word was brought to the Chairman of the Faculty, Professor Bonnycastle, that damage was being done to the books in the library room. The Chairman hurried to the Rotunda, sent for the Librarian, and learned that he had chosen that moment again to be absent from the University without leave. The Chairman took action of an unusual character. He suspended Brockenbrough from his office for two days, and appointed a substitute Librarian. This emergency action received the full approval of the Faculty.

The Faculty's confidence in Wertenbaker at this stage is indicated by its appointment of him on November 28 as Assistant Librarian. These moves had the effect of bringing Brockenbrough literally to book. They also encouraged further action on the pending report of Professor Emmet and his special committee. That committee had been directed to prepare a full set of resolutions concerning the Library. The resolutions were ready by the end of 1834, and were adopted by the Faculty on 9 January 1835. This time the Faculty threw the book at Brockenbrough. It was not in its power to remove him from his office permanently. But the resolutions bound him tightly to his library duties; and just prior to the meeting of the Visitors in July 1835, the Faculty approved of a resolution presented by Professor Emmet that the whole library matter be referred to the Board of Visitors. The Board, however, found also before it the resignation of William Brockenbrough; and so its only action was to accept the resignation and to reappoint Wertenbaker as Librarian.

Meantime Brockenbrough had already achieved the goal of his law degree. Since he was suffering to an increased extent from ill health, he decided to try the climate of the Territory, as it then was, of Florida. He settled in Tallahassee, and that became his home for fifteen years. He died in Tallahassee in 1850, at the early age of thirty-seven.

His career during those fifteen years in Florida must have been a matter of wonderment to those who had known him only as Librarian. He was admitted to the bar, advanced rapidly as a lawyer, served in turn as a member of the Florida House of Representatives and of the Florida Senate, was selected as President of the Senate, became a United States District Attorney, and upon the admission of Florida as a State was elected one of its first Representatives in the Congress of the United States.

This story began with a moral. It is well that for our estimate of Brockenbrough we have also the Florida conclusion. Yet that conclusion makes clear that the lack in his librarianship was not one of ability.

4. THOMAS BEVERLEY HOLCOMBE (1823-1872)
LIBRARIAN 1857-1861

The fourth Librarian, Thomas Beverley Holcombe, was like the third, William Henry Brockenbrough, closely related to a prominent member of the teaching and admin-

istrative staff of the University of Virginia. In the case of
the Brockenbroughs it was a father and son relationship. In
the case of the Holcombes it was the relationship of brothers. The two Holcombes (there were six brothers altogether)
came from a Lynchburg, Virginia, family which had a
distinguished ancestry. The brothers' great grandfather had
aided in the founding of Hampden-Sydney College, their
grandfather had been a Major in the Revolutionary War
and a Lieutenant Colonel in the War of 1812, and their
father was successful both as a physician and as an ordained
minister—the two professions being actively pursued simul-
taneously. The father and mother had become opposed to
slavery, had liberated their own slaves, and had removed
from Lynchburg to Indiana. Later, however, they had
returned to Virginia—this time the physical climate, not
the political one, being the deciding factor. In 1851 the
elder of the brothers, James Philemon Holcombe, had been
appointed Adjunct Professor of Law at the University of
Virginia and three years later had been promoted to a full
professorship. He was a vigorous supporter of States'
Rights; and in the years just prior to 1861 he became the
spokesman of the more extreme elements in the University.
On the outbreak of the war he resigned his chair in order
to devote his notable powers as lawyer, author, and pub-
licist to crusading projects in behalf of the Confederacy.

The younger brother, Thomas Berkeley Holcombe, was
of a more retiring disposition, with fewer of the qualities
of a crusader. He had been a student at the University of
Virginia, but only for one session, 1841-1842. He had gone
with his parents to Indiana, and had later settled in Cincin-
nati, Ohio. There he became associated with Alexander
McGoffey in a law office, his own special interest apparently
being the codification of law. Like the Professor of Law
and like another brother, William Henry Holcombe, who
attained to leadership among homeopathic physicians,

William Wertenbaker

Rector Jefferson's Letter of Appointment to William Wertenbaker

Thomas displayed facility in writing; and in time he took on the editorship of a democratic publication, the Indiana *State Journal*.

It was with this background that Thomas Holcombe became Librarian of the University of Virginia. In the preceding historical sketch it has been pointed out that he was the nearest approach to a "professional" Librarian that the University had during the nineteenth century. It will be remembered that in his four years in that office, from September 1857 through December 1861, there was increase in student enrollments and in the number of book purchases, and that there was added to the Librarian's regular duties the preparation of a catalogue. Holcombe was a diligent and a conscientious worker. This was probably fortunate for him—as well as for the University Library. For it was a time of bitter partisanship, in which his brother, the Professor of Law, was taking a leading part; and concentration on routine tasks would help to supply wholesome balance for the gentle and sensitive younger brother. Even so, it seems to have been an increasingly difficult period for Librarian Holcombe; and by October 1860 he was petitioning the Faculty to permit him to close the Library at noon on Saturday, in order that he might "spend as many Sundays as I conveniently can in Lynchburg, my birthplace and where many relatives and friends of my family reside." To compensate for the earlier closing, which would enable him to avoid traveling on the Sabbath Day, he offered to open the Library earlier on five days of the week. If the request were granted, he wrote to the Faculty, "I shall be able to do this without violating the Sabbath or neglecting my duties." And he pathetically added, "My health and spirits urgently require some relief of this sort." It is pleasant to record that the request was granted.

Had the times not been out of joint, it is possible that

Holcombe might have made a valuable contribution to the development of this University Library. But 1861 ended peace-time progress. In December of that year, Holcombe departed from the University on leave of absence for the balance of that session. He did not return.

Of his remaining years there is little known. His interest in literary studies seems to have continued. In 1870 there came from him to the Board of Visitors a letter asking for the loan of books from the University Library. But the policy of book loans had not yet been liberalized; and it was deemed necessary to reply to this former Librarian that he would be permitted the use of books in the library room only. In his last days he suffered increasingly from a persecution complex. Fortunately those days were spent in the friendly home in New Orleans of his physician brother, William Henry Holcombe; and there he died in December 1872. He had been a mild and kindly soul in a family of vigorous and dominant personalities and in a time of tragic emotional strain.

5. ROBERT RIDDICK PRENTIS (1818-1871)
ACTING LIBRARIAN 1861-1865

The place of Robert Riddick Prentis in the roll of Librarians is unlike that of any other incumbent of the office. He was not appointed by the Board of Visitors, but temporarily and as an emergency measure by the Faculty. His "charge of the Library" was an added and not a major part of his duties. During his four years as Acting Librarian, from December 1861 to July 1865, there were fewer student readers than at any other period in the history of the University of Virginia, the hours of opening were at a minimum, additions to the book collection were infrequent, and there were no purchases. Moreover there is not much uplift of spirit for those who have to remain at home during war time. Yet by faithful day-by-day performance of this additional duty of his, Acting Librarian Prentis was able not only to protect the Library but also to keep it in continuous use. If the influence of such a collection of books in such a period (or in any period) could be weighed, it would surely be found that this servant returned more than a talent hidden in the earth.

Robert Prentis came from a distinguished family in Nansemond County, Virginia, his paternal grandfather being Judge Joseph Prentis of Williamsburg and his maternal grandfather Col. Robert Moore Riddick of "Jericho" in Nansemond County. He was a student at the University of Virginia during the sessions 1838-1840, and was appointed Proctor and Patron in 1853, eight years before the wartime care of the Library was added to his responsibilities. In 1855 he was one of the guarantors for the cost of the erection at the University of Temperance Hall, others in the group being General Cocke, Professor Minor, and Librarian Wertenbaker. In addition to his varied duties during the war, he seems to have been a Collector of Internal Revenue for the Confederate Government. At the close of the war, the office of Proctor (the title Patron had been dropped in 1861) was temporarily suspended. But the services of Prentis were not long allowed to remain dormant, for in 1867 he was appointed Commissioner of Accounts, and he was continued in that office until his death on 23 November 1871. From November 1870 until his death he was also Clerk of Albemarle County. His years as an administrative officer thus covered periods of prosperity, of disaster, and of reconstruction.

Four years after his student days at the University, in 1844, Prentis married Margaret Ann Whitehead, and he was the father of twelve children. (He himself had ten brothers or sisters.) One of the twelve, Joseph Prentis, a Sergeant in the Confederate Army, was killed at the battle of Malvern Hill. Another, Robert Riddick Prentis II, became Chief Justice of the Virginia Supreme Court of Appeals. The Prentis home at the University was on "Monroe Hill"; and he is buried in the University Cemetery.

As in the case of John Vaughan Kean, there is a later link between Robert Prentis and the University and its Library. For the great great nephew of the Acting Librarian of 1861-1865, namely, Robert Henning Webb, was Professor of Greek at the University from 1912 to 1950, a member of the Faculty Library Committee from 1929 to 1950, and its Chairman, succeeding Dean Metcalf, from 1940 to 1950. An endowment fund for the purchase of books on Ancient Languages was in 1953 presented in his memory by friends and former students of Professor Webb.

6. WILLIAM AYLETT WINSTON (1827-1894)
LIBRARIAN 1882-1886

In strict order of appointment as Librarian, Frederick Winslow Page should follow William Wertenbaker's last "tour of duty." But as Page's first term, 1881-1882, was for one year only, and as the significant part of his service came during the twelve years from 1891 to 1903, it is more consistent with the historical development of the University Library to list him after Winston and Baker and before Patton.

It will be recalled that the abrupt termination in 1882 of Page's one year term had a political cause. William Winston was the Readjuster Librarian. He came in suddenly and he went out suddenly. His four years' tenure of the office was without special distinction. But such evidence as we have would indicate that the duties were performed with consistent carefulness and fidelity. He was concurrently Secretary of the Board of Visitors and Secretary of the Faculty, and the businesslike legibility of his record of the meetings of those two bodies is likely to elicit favorable comment from whoever has occasion to pore over the ponderous volumes of those university archives.

Winston had been a student at the University of Virginia during the session of 1850-1851. In his matriculation entry his date of birth is given as 23 November 1827 and his home as Hanover Court House, Virginia. Winstons had settled in Hanover County in colonial days, and by mid-nineteenth century there were several branches of the family, occupying such houses as Blenheim, Courtland, Manheim, Signal Hill, Wilton, and Woodland. Curiously enough, it has been difficult to establish with what branch of the family Librarian Winston was connected. Many of the Hanover County records were destroyed in 1865; and this William Winston himself has, no doubt quite unintentionally, been far from helpful. For at his matriculation, under the heading "Parent or Guardian," he simply wrote "Self." His own name, moreover, was entered merely as "Wm. A. Winston." It seems fairly certain, however, that he was the William Aylett Winston whose father, William Chamberlayne Winston, is recorded as having been born in 1802 and as having married Sarah Pollard. If so, the Librarian was of the seventh generation from the pioneer settler, William Winston.

To the established facts, the date of his birth, his connection with Hanover County, his one session as a student in the University, and his four years as University Librarian, we have from an early alumni record the additional items that he served in the Confederate Army and that he was at one time a clerk in the Virginia Legislature. We know also that not long after he was replaced as Librarian, he went to Minnesota. Three Winston brothers, who were cousins of his, had in the late 1870's established in Minneapolis a firm of railway contractors which was to have a large part in opening that region to railway communication.

Beginning in 1890 William Winston was for a couple of years a clerk in that company, and then he became Librarian of the Minneapolis Central High School. His death, apparently from cancer, came on 21 January 1894.

7. JAMES BISCOE BAKER (1834-1902)
LIBRARIAN 1886-1891

To replace William Winston the new Board of Visitors chose a schoolteacher from southwest Virginia, James Biscoe Baker.

Baker had been a student at the University of Virginia and a soldier in the Confederate Army. As a soldier he had taken part in only one battle, but in that he had displayed supreme courage. The story of his bravery under fire seems to have become widely known, and it may have been a contributing cause for this recognition by the Board of Visitors.

He had been born in Middleburg, Loudoun County, Virginia, 17 October 1834. He was seventeen when he matriculated at the University of Virginia, and he continued as a student for three sessions, 1851-1853 and 1855-1856. He was teaching in a school near Culpeper when the war broke out. A gentle and diffident youth, he seemed little fitted to be a soldier. Yet he enlisted in a cavalry company recruited in Loudoun, his home county, and he gained promotion to the rank of Orderly Sergeant.

The company was attached to the command of the dashing J. E. B. Stuart, then a Colonel. At the First Battle of Manassas, that company and another were ordered to dislodge a body of Northern soldiers concealed in some woods. Too late it was discovered that the hidden troops comprised a whole brigade. But the small Confederate force did not pause to reason why. The charge was made in the face of a withering fire. Sergeant Baker was hit in the knee, but he did not waver. A bullet broke his arm. Yet he still galloped on. Then his horse was killed under him, a shot pierced his body, and he was flung headlong on the ground. There he lay while the battle raged above him. Finally the Northern forces withdrew and the sorely wounded Sergeant could be given treatment by an army doctor. He was moved to a field hospital. The tale of his gallantry spread abroad, and Colonel Stuart sent him a personal letter of commendation, offering promotion and a place on the Colonel's staff. But it had been found necessary that his leg be amputated—and his army days were over.

In time Baker recovered, and went back to the milder disciplines of teaching. He found an opening in southwest Virginia and became the headmaster of a boys' school in Abingdon. It was while he was there that the offer came of the librarianship at his University.

He was appointed both Librarian and Secretary of the Faculty, but not Secretary of the Board of Visitors. Since Winston no Librarian has held the Visitors' secretaryship—that is, in the period covered by this history. As it happens, Baker was the last Librarian to be Secretary of the Faculty. He was also permitted, as Winston had been, to occupy a house "west of Dawson's Row." To this permission the Board of Visitors, who were keeping a tight rein on the finances, cautiously added: "but without any expenditure for repairs."

The five years of Baker's tenure of the office were not marked by untoward events—or by toward ones, for that matter. According to approximations recorded in the University Catalogues, the number of volumes increased from 48,000 to 50,000. The growth in student enrollment was more rapid, from 301 to 472. Baker had appreciation of the value of books and familiarity with the needs of students; and his duties were faithfully performed—though daily to the point of exhaustion because of his physical handicaps.

Meantime, in 1888, Frederick Page had been called back from the position he was occupying as Deputy Clerk of Albemarle County to fill a newly created office, that of Clerk to the Chairman of the Faculty. By 1891 it seemed wise again to make a separation of offices. This time Page was asked to resume the librarianship, and the offices of Secretary of the Faculty and Clerk to the Chairman were combined and offered to Baker, these two posts demanding from him less physical exertion. Baker continued to hold the dual secretaryships until his death on 21 November 1902.

While he was holding this double post, there was one more day in the old Sergeant's life when he was suddenly called upon for heroic effort. That was the day of the burning of the Rotunda. When news of the conflagration reached him, Baker, limping on his crutch, with desperate effort hurried to the office of the Secretary of the Faculty, which was in the lower part of the building, and there remained "against remonstrance until every record, every book, every paper in the office under his charge had been removed to a place of safety."

The quotation is from the master pen of Chairman Thornton and is taken from a moving article which was contributed to the *Alumni Bulletin* of April 1903, following Baker's death. To that article we owe much of what is known about this appealing figure. In it his character is thus summarized by the Chairman of the Faculty:—

For five years after his [Baker's] appointment as Secretary the writer came into daily and hourly contact with him. He learned thus to know his many admirable qualities, to realize the simplicity and sincerity of his nature, and to estimate at their true worth his lofty sense of duty and the genuine modesty of his spirit. He possessed but little power of initiative, and shunned responsibility when he could fitly avoid it. It was necessary to give a certain general guidance and direction to him in all his work. But his industry was unwearied, his fidelity unwavering. A perfectly loyal man, he was worthy of implicit trust, however delicate or however trivial the confidence; a perfectly sincere man, he never sought to cover up an error or hide a gap; a perfectly faithful man, he spared neither strength nor pains to finish his task and complete the work given him to do.

That was the simple and consistent story of a lifetime. On one day in his twenties and on another day when he was sixty-one, that deep-lying sense of responsibility and of obedience to command brought him face to face with violent emergencies. The change was in the circumstances, not in the character; and in those crises it was the resolution and latent heroism of a life of steadfast fidelity that stood revealed.

8. FREDERICK WINSLOW PAGE (1826-1913)
LIBRARIAN 1881-1882, 1891-1903

Since Frederick Winslow Page's first connection with the University of Virginia Library was prior to the librarianships of William Winston and James Baker, various details concerning him have already been given; namely, that he was appointed Assistant Librarian in 1876, that he succeeded William Wertenbaker as Librarian in 1881, that he was ousted by the Readjuster Board of Visitors in 1882, that he then became Deputy Clerk of Albemarle County, that he had been called back to the University in 1888 to fill the new office of Clerk of the Chairman of the Faculty, and that he was restored to the library post in 1891.

The popular conception of the genus Librarian, as illustrated at the Rotunda, must have been quite different in Page's day from what it had been at the beginning of the University. When Wertenbaker succeeded Kean, both were college students. When Page succeeded Wertenbaker, the latter was eighty-four years of age and the former fifty-five. The position had grown old with Wertenbaker; and at the time Frederick Page became a fledgling Librarian, he had already been a practicing lawyer, a newspaper publisher, a veteran artilleryman, and a farmer.

He came of a famous Virginia family. Dean James Morris Page and Professor Thomas Walker Page of the University of Virginia Faculty were nephews of his. Librarian Page's paternal grandfather was Major Carter Page of the Revolutionary Army, who married Mary Cary of Ampthill, Chesterfield County, her line running back to Pocahontas. His father was Mann Page, doctor of medicine, who lived at Keswick (sometimes called Turkey Hill) in Albemarle County, and who married Jane Frances Walker of nearby Castle Hill. He himself was born at the Turkey Hill estate on 20 November 1826. He was a student at the University of Virginia for the three sessions 1843-1846; and his "Random Reminiscences" of those days, as contributed to *College Topics* in 1909, were quoted by Philip Alexander Bruce in volume three of his *History of the University of Virginia*. Later he returned to the University for a fourth session, 1848-1849, this time for courses in law. In 1850 he married Anne Meriwether of Kinloch, Albemarle County, and settled in Lynchburg to practice law. Seven years later, however, he decided to move to Petersburg, and there he joined with Robert Bolling in publishing the *Petersburg Intelligencer*. News coverage had its limitations in those days, but subjects for editorial comment were plentiful. The *Intelligencer* supported John Bell in the presidential election of 1860. When war broke out, Page enlisted as a private in an Albemarle artillery company commanded by Captain William H. Southall, and he fought through the war. At its close there seemed little opportunity for law practice or newspaper publishing, and Page, with his wife and seven children, turned to farming for a reconstruction livelihood, so that when he was called in 1876 to aid in the custodianship of the University Library, he came like Cincinnatus from the plow.

At the Library he found a truly congenial vocation. Habits of reading and the ability to appreciate and judge what he read had been acquired in his college days; and he was uniformly helpful and encouraging in his contacts with student readers. The fine quality of his courtesy is stressed in contemporary references to his services as a Librarian. When he retired in 1903, the Faculty paid him a tribute from which a cogent passage may be quoted:—

His love of books, interest in literature, courteous manners, sense of order and intelligent appreciation of what the students needed in their search for information made him a person singularly well-fitted to hold this delicate and responsible office which always requires a combination of tact, patience, and skill. These were found united in Mr. Page.

The longer and more significant period of his librarianship, 1891 to 1903, was Januslike in effect. Catastrophically divided by the burning of the Rotunda, it looked backward to the Library founded by Jefferson and forward to the confused beginning of the present Library. Librarian Page was better qualified to be the last of the old than to be the first of the new. The services lauded by the Faculty were of course more capable of performance where order and personal knowledge of the books were assets. In Librarian Page's eight years after the Rotunda fire the conditions were of constant confusion and of a rapid but poorly assimilated influx of gift books. Of modern technical aids there was practically none. Under the pressure of daily circulation demands, Page had no leisure to prepare such aids—and it is indeed doubtful whether he had much conception of their nature and value. Moreover the years had taken a toll of his physical strength. The steadiness and courteous character of his service were maintained, but there came to be a shadow of discouragement over his part in the new Library.

During the ten years between his retirement in 1903

and his death on 27 February 1913, Frederick Page continued to live in Charlottesville, and he became, as an article in the *Alumni News* expressed it, "one of the most familiar figures of the past generation of students." His wife had died in 1867, and he had in 1883 married Lucy Cook Beale of Fredericksburg, a sister of the wife of Professor Dunnington of the University Faculty. She died in 1897. Page married a third time in 1902. His third wife, Lucy White Bryan of Memphis, Tennessee, survived him. There were seven children by the first marriage, but none by the second and third. In view of the lack of library aids that so sorely handicapped service after the Rotunda fire, there has been peculiar appropriateness in the establishment in 1947 by his youngest child, Miss Mildred Page, of a fund in his memory, the income to be used for the purchase of books on librarianship and its techniques.

9. JOHN SHELTON PATTON (1857-1932)
LIBRARIAN 1903-1927

Of these nine Librarians of the first hundred years, eight had to do with the first university library collection, before the burning of the Rotunda. Frederick Page knew that collection in its latest and fullest form. He also saw the beginning of the second and present-day collection. But it was the ninth of the group, John Shelton Patton, whose concern was exclusively with the new collection. In this respect he stood alone.

He was like the other eight, however, in being a native of Virginia, and like them he had been a student at the University of Virginia. Patton was born in Augusta County, near Staunton, on 10 January 1857. His father lost his life as a soldier in the Confederate Army, and the boy was cared for by a devoted aunt. He attended schools in Waynesboro and Charlottesville, and was a student at the University of

Virginia for three sessions, 1877-1880. In 1881 he married Beatrice Faber and moved to Salem, Virginia, where he became editor of the *Roanoke Times,* a newspaper which opposed the Readjuster Party. Two years later he returned to Charlottesville to take an editorial position on the *Jeffersonian Republican.* Connection with that newspaper continued until 1894, when Patton, who had meantime served as a member of the City Council, became Mayor of Charlottesville. At the close of his term as Mayor, in 1896, he joined with James H. Lindsay, under the firm name of Lindsay and Patton, to take over the publication of the *Daily Progress,* which had absorbed the *Jeffersonian Republican.* In March 1899, however, Patton terminated active connection with newspaper publishing and entered the employment of the University of Virginia. For several years he had been a member of the Charlottesville School Board, and during the early part of his connection with the University he was Superintendent of the City Schools. His first post at the University appears to have been in connection with an advertising committee formed by the Board of Visitors after the burning of the Rotunda. He was also for a year or so Secretary of the General Alumni Association. Then came the appointment as Assistant Librarian, followed a year later by Patton's succession to the librarianship. He was then forty-six years of age.

In the historical sketch of the University Library details have been given concerning the main products of Patton's twenty-four years in the library vocation—the augmented importance of the position of Librarian, the development of a Library Staff, the extension in amount and in forms of service, the growth and diffusion of the collections, the new attack on the problems of classification and cataloguing, and the emphasis on needs, particularly the need of a new library building. The unavoidable emphasis on needs dimmed the enthusiasm which marked the library effort at the beginning of President Alderman's administration, and, as no Alladin's lamp could be discovered, the later of the twenty-four years tended to be a dulled maintenance of an unsatisfactory *status quo*. But Patton's previous experience as a writer and as a civic leader afforded outlets for effort and relief from confining routine throughout his librarianship; and to complete the story of his career there should be some record of the impressive by-products from these avocations of his.

He was recognized as a leading citizen of Charlottesville, and his counsel continued to be sought in civic affairs. He served as a member of the Board of Appointments for the Miller Manual Labor School of Albemarle County, he was a trustee of the Charlottesville Home for the Aged, and when Charlottesville acquired a Public Library through the generosity of Paul Goodloe McIntire, Patton was for a term Chairman of its Board of Trustees.

His entrance into the library field naturally brought into play the habits acquired as a reporter and editorial writer. His first library efforts were to try to bring order out of the confused conditions still prevailing in the Rotunda. Herein was the material for the summer quarter courses in Library Methods and also for a group of lectures on general library subjects which he offered through the University's Extension Division. He found congenial occupation in the preparation of library reports, in the establishment of a library bulletin, in the composition of a library handbook, and in the compilation of bibliographical data.

Such activities were by no means limited to library subjects. He was a member of the Editorial Committee of the *Alumni Bulletin* from 1913 until that publication was discontinued in 1924. To it he contributed over a score of signed articles on such diverse subjects as the Old Swan Tavern, John S. Mosby, George Rogers Clark, Thomas

Jefferson's Contributions to Natural Science, and the University of Virginia in the [First] World War. Scattering articles of his appeared also in other publications and in his old newspaper, the Charlottesville *Daily Progress*.

There are also a half dozen books bearing his name as author or editor. Early in his connection with the University, before he became Librarian, he and Sallie J. Doswell had compiled the useful handbook, *The University of Virginia: Glimpses of its Past and Present*. That was in 1900. A second and much altered edition of this, with a third collaborator, Lewis D. Crenshaw, was issued in 1915 with a new title, *Jefferson's University: Glimpses of the Past and Present of the University of Virginia*. Patton's history of the University, *Jefferson, Cabell and the University of Virginia*, was published in 1906. Three years later he was associated with Professor Charles William Kent in editing the volume entitled *The Book of the Poe Centenary. The Poems of John R. Thompson: with a Biographical Introduction*, which was published by Scribner in 1920, was perhaps his most important literary contribution. It received highly favorable reviews by Dean John Calvin Metcalf and Historian Philip Alexander Bruce. In 1925 he collaborated again with Sallie J. Doswell in a book on *Monticello and its Master*. A revised edition of this appeared in 1930. In the year of his retirement as Librarian, 1927, sundry poems of his were collected and issued with the title, *Love and Mistress Annabel and Other Verses*.

His career as Librarian extended two years into the second century of the Library's history. The Virginia State Law had by that time made retirement compulsory at the age of three score and ten. This law had not previously been in force, so that Frederick Page had remained Librarian until he was seventy-seven and William Wertenbaker until he was eighty-four. Patton continued to live in Charlottesville, not far from the University, until his death 1 October

1932. He had been appointed Librarian in the year before Doctor Alderman became President of the University. He passed away in the year after Alderman's death. Both at the time of Patton's retirement and at the time of his death, resolutions commending his efforts were voted by the Board of Visitors. In the former, Patton's services to the University Library were fittingly described as having been rendered "with devotion, high purposes, and good results."

The Alderman Library, a pedestrian's view

The Alderman Library viewed from a plane

VI

The First Quarter
of the Second Century
1925-1950

1. GRAPHS OF THE UNIVERSITY AND THE
LIBRARY

T HE QUARTER CENTURY that began the second hundred years of the University of Virginia was close-packed with an exhausting succession of economic and political events: an extravagant boom in the United States, a worldwide financial depression, a global war, and an aftermath in which hope of peace faded before an ideological struggle between fundamentally opposed conceptions of the rights of man. The University of Virginia, like other institutions of higher learning, was a microcosm reflecting those changes. The closing years of President Alderman's administration proved to be a harvest time for material growth. His sudden death in 1931 spared him from a financial winter in which his friend and successor, John Lloyd Newcomb, strained the powers of the human spirit in the effort to conserve. Against the foundation thus preserved swept the tornado of the second world war, turning the University once more into a training camp. Discerning statesmanship, the salutary effect of which may become increasingly evident in the decades to follow, saved the benefits of education for that wartime generation of American youth, and, on the cessation of the fighting, flooded the Universities with students notably above the average in maturity and diligence. When President Newcomb retired in 1947, his successor, Colgate Whitehead Darden, Jr., the third President of the University, continued the development of the material resources of the University, with the aim of a more adequate girding for concentration on the primary functions of a State University; namely, to preserve the people's heritage and to contribute to the advancement and the diffusion of knowledge, with steadfast belief, in the familiar Jeffersonian words, that enlightenment of the people and the quickening of its hostility to every form of tyranny are essential for the preservation of free government and human liberty.

The story of library development through this quarter of a century differs from the story of the first hundred years. In the first hundred years, the Library, after a promising start, fell into a minor role; and the graph of its progress follows closely the rise and fall in the fortunes of the University. By contrast, in the twenty-five years from 1925 to 1950 the university and the library developments were not parallel. A graph of the University's history for those years would somewhat resemble the fluctuating register of earth tremors on a seismograph; while a graph of library development would take the form of a steady and accelerating curve upward. The University's first decade of boom altitudes followed by valleys of financial retrenchment was for the Library a period of lowly struggle over a consistently rough course. There did emerge, however, an early gleam of hope. Then, while the University was still plunged in the depths of the economic depression, that first essential for the betterment of the library service, a new building for the general library, was secured. Thereafter, through the shooting war and the cold war, the course of the University remained variable, but with an upturn at the close. As for the Library, though there were delays and disappointments, its progress continued resolutely towards something like the combined undergraduate and research service that was the goal. By 1950, therefore, the University Library was at long last beginning to resume the stature which Jefferson's vision and personal efforts had established for it in 1825.

The telling of the story of this quarter of a century also takes a different form. The earlier record is an historical sketch, written from the outside. In this last section, the writer himself had a part in the action, and there is unavoidably a subjective approach—the story tends to be a report rather than a history. Perhaps the most visible indication that this is a personal narrative is in the frequent manifestation of the tenth Librarian's pride in his associates. The confession of this pride is made to the reader at the outset of this sixth section, not in apology, but as an early clue to the chief cause of such success as has attended this quarter century of effort.

2. BEGINNINGS OF REORGANIZATION

The foregoing are general statements. Now, as a radio commentator might say, for some of the details. The 101st session of the University of Virginia began in 1925. There were then, including the Law Librarian, seven full time members of the Library Staffs; and in the general library in the Rotunda and in the thirteen separate collections scattered among the university buildings there was a reported total of 131,422 volumes. With the exception of the 17,194 which had survived the fire of 1895, this was a new collection which had been assembled in thirty years.

John Shelton Patton continued to be Librarian through two years of the second century. During that biennium there was little alteration in the *status quo* of the years immediately preceding. There was completion of the process of taking over the northwest wing of the Rotunda building as a stack and reading room for periodicals; from James Reese McKeldin came an endowment fund of $1,000 for books in Philosophy; an additional $1,000 for the Education Library was received from Alfred William Erickson; the Thomas Carroll Smith Memorial Endowment Fund of $10,000 was established for the Law Library; and 1926 saw the beginning of the Institute for Research in the Social Sciences, organized and headed by Professor Wilson Gee. That Institute had significance for library development because of the augmented emphasis on research and because of the effective cooperation between Professor Gee and the University Library in matters of common concern.

Meantime, as a step toward an expanded library programme, Dean Metcalf, Chairman of the Faculty Library Committee, had turned his attention to the selection of a successor to Librarian Patton. It was deemed wise this time to choose someone with previous library experience. Jefferson's conception of the Librarian as a guardian and a guide was, in fact, being broadened to include the Librarian as an administrator. The choice would naturally have fallen on an alumnus of the University of Virginia, as it had in all previous cases. But librarianship as a vocation appeared to have been singularly lacking in appeal to the University's graduates. It therefore seemed necessary to widen the field of search. Chairman Metcalf's own realization of the difficulties in the situation that the new Librarian must face was sharpened by the unwillingness of several of those who were under favorable consideration to undertake the task. Actually it was not until the month after Librarian Patton's retirement that the new appointment was made; and then, after the century of ingrowing selections, the choice went amusingly far afield. For it fell on Harry Clemons, who had been Librarian of the missionary University of Nanking in China until March of that year, 1927, when a Russian-induced civil uprising had led to the historic "Nanking Incident" and had made necessary the evacuation of Americans from that section of China. Chairman Metcalf learned of the possible availability of the Nanking Librarian, arranged for a conference as soon as the latter returned to the United States, and the appointment was made by President Alderman early in July, with approval somewhat later by the Board of Visitors.

The new Librarian, wishing to enroll in a refresher course in Library Administration at Columbia University that summer (a course conducted by that Solon among Librarians, Azariah Root of Oberlin College), did not take office until September, Miss Dinwiddie, the Assistant Librarian, being in charge during the intervening months. In addition to this special library course at Columbia, the tenth Librarian in the series had had academic training at Wesleyan, Princeton, and Oxford Universities and library and teaching experience at Wesleyan, Princeton, and Nanking. During the first world war he had been the official representative of the American Library Association in charge of the library war service for the American Expeditionary Force in Siberia; and for a brief period he had been connected with the Chinese Section of the Library of Congress. It would appear to have been a daring gamble on the part of President Alderman and Chairman Metcalf to interpret such types of experience as applicable to the situation at the University of Virginia.

The obvious first moves for the newcomer were to familiarize himself as rapidly as possible with the details of the situation, to coordinate his efforts with those of the small Staff which had been loyally maintaining the service schedules, and to develop his own planning in harmony with the purposes and policies of the Faculty Library Committee. In his first report, covering the last four months of 1927, there is record of several minor moves that would not impede a service in operation, of a listing of the accumulation of unfinished tasks, of an increase in the cataloguing force, and of an extension of the hours of opening from forty-nine to eighty-four a week. The actual addition to the hours of opening had, however, been less extensive than the figures indicated. In the previous session a small group of students, headed by Joseph Lee Vaughan and Hubert Douglas Bennett, had been permitted to keep the library room open at night without pay, and such volunteer hours had not been included in the official figures. An early move of the new Librarian had been to arrange for salary compensation for this public-spirited service.

As for the actual extent of the University's holdings, a shelf by shelf count had been made of all library books in any way available in any building of the University. The total of this census, 151,333, did not include sundry unopened boxes of gifts or the motley aggregation of unprocessed volumes that covered the floor of the top gallery of the Rotunda. As there had been additions during the biennium 1925 to 1927, this total indicated the approximate correctness of the figure, 131,422, reported in 1925.

The increase in the Cataloguing Staff made it possible to give immediate attention to the century-old problem of cataloguing. In order that this might proceed as wisely as possible, half hour daily conferences of the Cataloguers were instituted; and it is doubtful if the four volume *Survey of Libraries in the United States,* which had been published by the American Library Association the previous year, proved anywhere more timely than it did for the little group in one of the first floor oval rooms in the Rotunda which daily read aloud and, with growing confidence and good humor and enthusiasm, discussed the problems encountered and the solutions attempted by other libraries.

128

Any glimmerings of enthusiasm were salutary. That patience was a primary requisite in the library programme at the University of Virginia had been and continued to be only too plainly apparent. Yet patience and the note of hope proved hardy, as was indicated three years later in the opening sentence of the library report for 1930:—

The activities of the Library Staff have resembled the efforts of a mountain climber. The path has led upward, but progress has been increasingly hampered by the crowding in of trees and under-brush. Occasional glimpses of a broadening prospect have stimulated the climber to renewed exertions; and the dishevelment and discomfort which attend such efforts have been borne with cheerfulness because of the hope that the goal can be reached.

It proved fortunate that the advance could be by several paths. For progress was possible on some even when others seemed at least temporarily blocked. A new home for the general library was essential. But there were also the problems of cataloguing, of collection building, and of assembling an adequate and efficient staff. None of these four was an end in itself. But each afforded an important means toward a fuller library service. Each will be considered in turn.

First, however, there should be a word concerning changes in the status of the Librarian and in the operations of the Faculty Library Committee.

The tenth Librarian was the first to be granted faculty rank, that of a Professor; and he became not only Secretary of the Faculty Library Committee but also a voting member. In the matter of initiative in library planning, Chairman Metcalf played the part of a wise parent: first directing the course of action, with careful explanation of the reasons therefor; then, as indications of maturity emerged, falling in behind as supporter and counsellor. A significant recognition of the new role of the Librarian as an administrator came in an invitation in October 1930 to present to the

University Senate a statement of the library situation and of proposed plans for reorganization. The Senate was a new body which had been established in 1926, its membership consisting of ten administrative officers and of eleven representatives elected by the Faculties of the various Departments. The reception accorded to the Librarian by this body was a far cry from the early attitude towards the student Librarians.

There was a gradual change also in the operations of the Faculty Library Committee. In course of time its function became more exclusively the formulation of general policies and not executive action. For several years after 1927 the responsibility for the selection of books to be purchased, which previously had involved the committee in its most time consuming task, had been continued. But by common consent that function was then transferred to an executive subcommittee composed of the Chairman and the Librarian. In order that authoritative knowledge of the material in each field of learning might be available, each School or Department—there were then approximately thirty in all—was asked to designate one of its faculty members to act in liaison with the Librarian and to pass on all requests for the purchase of books which might originate in his School or Department. This large group did not operate as a committee, and no meetings of the whole were ever attempted. But it did afford direct access between the Faculties and the Library; and in a number of cases it resulted in thoroughgoing attempts at collection building in the specified fields of learning that would have met the approval of Mr. Jefferson.

In the intensive planning for the proposed new building, especially in 1931 and 1938, and again in 1944 when attention was turned to plans for an extension to that building, the Library Committee performed much close and careful work through subcommittees, the Chairman and the Librarian being members of each subcommittee. In 1942 a subcommittee composed of Dean Metcalf, who had in 1940 been designated Chairman Emeritus of the Faculty Library Committee, of Professor Robert Henning Webb, the new Chairman, and of the Librarian made an extensive survey of the library operations in order to outline moves toward economy and efficiency, its proposals being afterwards approved by the whole committee.

As a result of its concentration on its policy making function, fewer meetings of the Library Committee became necessary, but each meeting was of augmented importance. In illustration of the actions taken, two examples may be given, one concerning censorship, the other the policy for acquisitions to the library collections.

Because of the nationwide agitation concerning censorship preliminary to the second world war, the Faculty Library Committee in December 1939

> voted its hearty and unanimous approval of the policy of impartially collecting and making available for research by qualified scholars materials on all sides of all questions, however controversial, thus avoiding such practices, either negative or positive, as would tend to render the Library an agency in the dissemination of propaganda.

The crucial words "for research by qualified scholars" are a signboard of the progress that had by that time been achieved in the development of the research service of this University Library.

The second action was the outcome of meetings held in April 1940, one having the unique character of being a joint session of the Faculty Library Committee with ten representatives of the Library Staff. The matter under consideration was the problem whether this Library should accept and make available all obtainable books, periodicals, pamphlets, newspapers, and manuscripts, or should adopt a policy of selection. There was final agreement on the following resolutions:—

That because of restriction of shelf space and of the funds necessary for making material available, it be recognized that the University Library is unable to undertake unlimited acceptance of printed and manuscript materials. That it is, however, desirable that every precaution be taken in the processes of rejection of materials; and that there is justification for the simple formula: 'When in doubt, retain.' That the Library Committee approve of the methods now being used by the Library Staff for the careful examination of all incoming and outgoing items; and that it recommend that the Library Staff call upon members of the Library Committee and of the University Faculty as a whole whenever assistance in such examination seems advisable.

Furthermore, that the Library Committee approve the policy of cooperation with other Libraries and of utilization of such means of obtaining materials as union catalogues, inter-library loans, and photostatic reproduction; and as a support to such policy, that it recommend the extension of the general reference and bibliographical collections in the Alderman Library as rapidly as funds may permit.

It needs but a reminder of the detailed supervision of all phases of library activity maintained by the Faculty Library Committees of the earlier years to reveal the contrast in the very wording of these resolutions.

This is, however, getting ahead of our story; and we return to the four paths of progress.

3. THE ALDERMAN LIBRARY BUILDING

It will be recalled that some doubt of the adequacy of the Rotunda for library purposes began to be whispered as early as the comparatively prosperous days of the 1850's; and that this had found full utterance in the years immediately preceding the Rotunda fire. The extension of the library space in the restoration of the Rotunda stilled those voices for a time. But by the end of the first hundred years they had been raised again, this time swelling to the volume of a chorus. It is true that there persisted some opposition to any move from the building Mr. Jefferson had planned for the Library. To this adherence to tradition the persuasive reply was made that, while the Founder's vision of the University included architectural design, it was essentially a vision of the spirit, not of bricks and mortar; and that whenever walls should tend to become a prison, there seemed no shadow of doubt that he would have impatiently and resolutely led the way towards freedom.

There was still to be a tedious wait for the new building. But now the planning for it began in earnest. Several possible sites were considered. A wooded dell, just across the road by the University Chapel, offered several advantages. It was on the axis of the Rotunda and only about a hundred and forty yards distant from it; the erection in 1929 of Monroe Hall and of eight dormitory units and the plans for additional construction to the westward gave assurance that this site would be still fairly central for the University; and the fifty-five foot dip made possible a structure which, by extending downward from the surface level, would achieve the needed floor space without towering above the low Jeffersonian buildings which it would face.

When virtual agreement on this site had been reached, thorough study was made of the present library needs of the University and of possible future needs, as far as they could be discerned, the whole Faculty being circularized for ideas. Extensive records of similar investigations at Dartmouth College and at Princeton University were secured and carefully scanned; blue prints of new buildings at Dartmouth and at the University of Rochester were studied; visits were made to other Libraries; and an experimental—and very amateur—set of specifications was drawn up and sent for criticism to the Librarians of several institutions which had recently erected new library buildings.

These Librarians proved most generous in giving aid, and the replies were noteworthy for frank and constructive criticism. Another timely library publication—James Thayer Gerould's *The College Library Building: Its Planning and Equipment*—proved particularly suggestive, especially in the matter of equipment. The final result of many months of effort was that a concisely stated but comprehensive set of specifications was made ready for submission to the future Architect of the new building.

In a double sense—both as to site and to financial history —this was a matter of erection in a depression. In 1924, when President Alderman "dreamed a few dreams" among which was "a great new library costing a million dollars," the times were flush. So were they during the first months of the intensive study on plans. That study, however, stressed both needs and economy. By 1929 it was possible for the Librarian to present to the Faculty Library Committee a detailed report. At the close of the presentation he was asked what all this would cost. His answer was specific: "On the basis of cubic contents at present prices the building will cost approximately a million dollars; and a second million will be needed for endowment." The silence that ensued was suddenly broken by President Alderman, who with a characteristic gesture removed his eyeglasses with one hand, placed the other firmly on the table before him, and announced: "Gentlemen, I have finished with consideration of thirty-seven dollars and fifty cents!"

It is significant that as President Alderman's imagination thus caught fire, it flashed back to thoughts of the Founder. In his address before the University on Jefferson Day, 13 April 1931, there came these ringing words:—

The need of a great library building, which by its spaciousness and beauty may stand before the world as a symbol of the worth and dignity of learning, is the supreme requirement of this University at this stage of its work, on purely university levels.

Equal to the need of a great structure is the need of an adequate endowment for its operations. The sum of money necessary to realize these needs will approximate two million dollars. I must reserve for some future time the detailed objectives in this large undertaking, and the many vital reasons why it must be achieved; but every son and friend of the University must know that this is the most fundamental and significant purpose determined upon since Jefferson laid out on this green hill top the Rotunda, the Lawns, and the Ranges. . . The very angels in heaven might well envy men and women who have the power and the desire to set free the forces that inhere in this intention. Personally my own *nunc dimittis* will ring out with pride if the glory should fall to me of beholding the lines of this endeavor assume form and substance.

Such beholding by President Alderman was not to be. That was his last address before the University. Later that same month, on April twenty-ninth, he died from a cerebral hemorrhage while on his way to take part in the inaugural ceremonies for Harry Woodburn Chase as President of the University of Illinois. The administration of the University of Virginia was carried on, first as Acting President and two years later as President, by John Lloyd Newcomb, who had been Dean of the Department of Engineering since 1925 and Assistant to the President since 1926. President Newcomb, like Dean Metcalf, had been among the first to realize that a new library building was vital for the development of the University. To that realization were now added his loyalty to his late leader and his determination to carry through this predominant purpose of Doctor Alderman's latest years—it being tacitly assumed that the proposed building should bear the name of the first President. By his patience, undismayed persistence, and skillful timing in this endeavor, President Newcomb revealed himself to be of the stock of the Founder.

However, in 1931 and for several years thereafter, the solicitation of funds from the State or from private donors was akin to the proverbial squeezing of juice from a cork.

The world depression was at its nadir. Yet in this very situation was found the cure, even as "out of the nettle, danger, we pluck the flower, safety." For in 1935 President Newcomb proposed that appeal be made to the Federal Emergency Agency of the Public Works Administration. This move was promptly supported by the Faculty Library Committee, and received the approval of the Board of Visitors. Permission was then granted by the Governor, George Campbell Peery, that formal petition be presented to the Public Works Administration. That body passed upon the project as being "economically sound and socially desirable." But the requirements by the Federal Government had meantime been altered so as to remove any likelihood of a grant for the total sum. There remained, however, the possibility of obtaining thus a portion of the necessary amount. President Newcomb and the Visitors thereupon canvassed the prospects of raising the required balance. The Rector of the Board of Visitors, Frederic William Scott, was from eminent experience as a financier a valuable counsellor in such proceedings. The method finally adopted was a bond issue secured by a student library fee covering a considerable period of years. The plan was to aim at a total of $950,000, of which fifty-five percent or $523,000 was to be obtained by the bond issue and forty-five percent or $427,909 was to be requested from the Public Works Administration. The application was made. But the operations of that Administration were by that time beginning to taper off, grants were being made more slowly, and the anxiety was intensified as the prospects of success faded.

Meantime it had been necessary to take hurried action in obtaining blueprint drawings to accompany the request. The application to the Governor for permission to present the petition had been illustrated by sketches of obviously homemade variety. At that point R. E. Lee Taylor, an alumnus of the University and the senior member of the architectural firm of Taylor and Fisher of Baltimore, volunteered to prepare the proper drawings. His offer was accepted, and he was later designated as the Architect of the new Library. That the specifications were ready for him proved of double value: for they both helped to expedite the Architect's work and also to insure full consideration at this strategic moment of an interior adapted to functional library use.

Public interest in the proposed new building had gradually been intensified, the credit in no small measure going to the Managing Editor, William Hillman Wranek, Jr., of the *Alumni News,* and to editorial writers in various newspapers in the State. Moreover, a searching appraisal of American Universities by Edwin Rogers Embree in an article in the June 1935 issue of the *Atlantic Monthly* had caused acute discomfort at the University of Virginia; and before this, in 1930, the erection of a football stadium had, by an ironical twist, stirred a marked reaction in favor of the library cause. In January 1936, at a largely attended meeting of the Washington Alumni, President Newcomb replaced the customary greetings from the University Administration by a forceful presentation of the urgency of the library situation. The Virginia Senators and Representatives and other officials in Washington joined with him in watchful waiting for a favorable moment in which to press for action on this university project. On September third Senator Glass and President Newcomb seized such a moment by a vigorous presentation to Harold Ickes, Secretary of the Interior and Administrator of Public Works. At 11:44 on the morning of Saturday, September twelfth, the message came through that the P.W.A. grant had been made. At 11:50 a telegram was dispatched to the Architect in Baltimore to start full operations at top speed; and President Newcomb then joined in an impromptu celebration by the Library Staff under the colonnade east of the

Rotunda, at which the dignified Chairman of the Faculty Library Committee, Dean Metcalf, gave memorable stamp to the spirit of the occasion by executing an extraordinary clog dance.

From this point events moved amain. The contract for excavations on the chosen site was awarded on November tenth, and the contract for the foundations on November twenty-first. During 1937 and the early part of 1938 other contracts were formally awarded, making fifteen in all, of which twelve went to Virginia firms. It is pleasant to record that something of the enthusiasm which was felt at the University for this undertaking was caught by a number of the contracting firms and their performance went beyond the letter of their contracts. Actual work on the excavations started late in November 1936. So did the rains—and the next twelvemonth ranks high in the Albemarle County records of precipitation. It proved necessary to postpone the completion date of the construction and equipment tasks from January to March 1938. But by April it was possible to move into the new building.

Difficulties had meantime emerged in the issuance of the bonds because of the wording of State laws, which were found so to limit the sale of the bonds that they could be purchased only by the Federal Government. But by good fortune a special session of the Virginia Legislature had been summoned for December 1936, and permission was obtained that consideration of the broadening of the pertinent act be included in the special session deliberations. Legislative approval was thus secured, and the bonds were successfully issued in January 1937.

The dispersion of the library collections had been augmented during the increasingly crowded conditions from 1925 to 1938, and eight additional libraries had come into being outside of the Rotunda, making a total of twenty-two in seventeen other buildings—a situation that administratively tended less to cultivation of the higher branches than to development of the lower limbs. The problem of deciding which collections should be moved into the new building was carefully considered by a subcommittee of the Faculty Library Committee in conference with each interested group. As a result the three department libraries (using department in the connotation customary at the University of Virginia), Engineering, Law, and Medicine, and ten laboratory or special collections, Astronomy, Chemistry, Fine Arts, Geology, the Institute for Research in the Social Sciences, Mathematics, Music, Physics, Public Administration, and Rural Social Economics, remained outside—though from eight of these certain classes of books were transferred to the Alderman Library.

The actual moving required twenty-seven working days, beginning with April twentieth and ending with May twenty-sixth. The abundance of terraces necessitated much carrying, and specially constructed and numbered boxes with handles were used, so that the classification order of the books could be preserved and volumes urgently needed could be located at all stages. By careful organization it was possible to keep the main reading rooms undisturbed except for one day, May tenth; and on the eleventh the new building was opened to readers. The first book that had been transferred to the Alderman Library was Doctor Alderman's memorial address on Woodrow Wilson, and this had been proudly carried by Miss Dinwiddie, the senior member of the Staff in length of service. When the doors were opened on the morning of May eleventh, President Newcomb was the first borrower, and his selection was the little volume of Doctor Alderman's response to a toast on Virginia. There were occasional delays in locating books during those first days. But Miss Roy Land, the Circulation Librarian, treated difficulty as adventure—and that spirit was transfused into both readers and library assistants.

The formal dedication of the Alderman Library was held on 13 June 1938 in connection with the final exercises of the 113th session of the University. President Newcomb made announcement of several donations, including that of the Tracy W. McGregor Library, an acquisition of extraordinary importance for development of research; and Dr. Dumas Malone delivered a notable dedicatory address. Doctor Malone was at that time Director of the Harvard University Press. He had formerly been Editor of the *Dictionary of American Biography,* and, previous to that, from 1923 to 1929, Professor of American History at the University of Virginia. There was special fitness in his presence on that occasion, for he was the biographer of President Alderman, and he had, in his years at the University of Virginia, been an active member of the Faculty Library Committee.

The new building thus dedicated and opened for use was a massive structure with a frontage of approximately two hundred feet and a depth of one hundred and seventy feet. By closing the northern side, it completed the quadrangle formed by West Range, Monroe Hall, Peabody Hall, and the Biological Laboratory. Facing these other buildings it was appropriately two stories in height. But the dip in the site permitted a five story elevation on the northern facade, and a ten story stack, there being two stack decks to a floor. The exterior design of both the southern and the northern facades was a three axis combination, in which a long central mass with a moderately elevated slate roof dominated the end wings and was joined to them by unaccented connecting links. The east and west wings were broken by two slightly projecting pavilions, between the pavilions being a row of engaged columns rising from the level of the fourth or main floor. As in the dominating type of University of Virginia buildings, there were two exterior colors, white for the columns, pilasters, cornices, and trim, and a pleasingly mottled brick red for the plain wall surfaces.

Within the new structure were two light courts, somewhat like the spaces in a thickly stemmed letter B. These were designed to afford light and ventilation—though it was later discovered that under a noonday summer sun they tended to become pockets of warm air. The unusual amount of exterior wall which resulted from these light courts had a supplementary advantage, since there was afforded so ample a support to the floors that the need for interior supporting walls was thereby largely eliminated. The room spaces could therefore be altered, as future needs might arise, by the simple erection or removal of partitions. The problem of future developments was also effectively met by the rectangular shape of the new building, as contrasted with the confining circle of the Rotunda; and along with the original plans there were also drawn tentative plans for a five story addition to the northward, which would greatly extend the available floor space.

As it was, the uniformly low height of the rooms, fifteen feet or twice the seven feet, six inches, of the standard stack deck, gave to the Alderman Library an unusual floor area, about 132,800 square feet, in proportion to a gross cubage of 2,102,000 cubic feet. The effort to gain maximum space for readers and staff and books was an outcome of the difficulties in administering more than a score of scattered collections. The absence of lofty, monumental effects was also specifically planned in order that both readers and books should be in homelike surroundings—a cardinal aim in the planning for the new general library.

The one exception was the monumental character of the entrance hall—a memorial to the first President. This had the height of two stories. The entrance was at the center of the southern facade and was therefore protected in winter and open to the prevailing breezes of summer. (There was only one other entrance to the building, leading into the receiving room for materials and located at the north end of the bottom floor of the west wing.) In the entrance hall the comfortable chairs, the displays of new books and of books of current interest, and the wall exhibition cases for special and constantly varied exhibits offered welcome to visitors. This was also a functional room, containing the circulation desk and the public card catalogue—which was planned to become a union catalogue for all books in possession of the University. On the same main floor (actually the fourth floor of the building) were located the spacious general reading room, with a reference collection shelved on wall cases, the general and circulation and reference offices, a room for national and special catalogues, and a workroom for the Preparations or Cataloguing Division. Thus the main floor served the general reader and afforded conveniently located headquarters for three of the five divisions of the Staff, Preparations, Circulation, and Reference.

On the floor below were rooms largely used by students: the reserved book reading room, a document reading room, a browsing room, and a room for current newspapers and magazines; there were also the offices of the extension library services, and a special room featuring the Garnett home library. On the quiet fifth floor above were studies for research scholars and small seminars for graduate student classes and conferences.

Grouped in another way, the eastern wing emphasized reading rooms and the western wing workrooms for the Staff. The reading room for rare books and manuscripts was on the second floor of the east wing, directly below the reserved book reading room; and still farther down, on the first floor, was a photographic laboratory for microfilm and photostatic reproductions. That equipment and the various gadgets scattered through the building would doubtless have intrigued Mr. Jefferson. As for the west wing, the processing of new materials began at the receiving room on the first floor, passed through the acquisition operations on the second floor, and on up to the main floor. On the receiving room floor at the bottom there was also a staff room, furnishing equipment and comfortable conditions for noonday lunches, for resting periods, for first aid in case of illness, and for occasional social gatherings of the Staff.

Other spaces within the new building—such as the series of functional offices and workrooms, five in each of the unaccented connecting links between the bookstack and the wings on the northern side—have not been enumerated. But what have been mentioned may sufficiently demonstrate the expansion of accommodations for readers and Library Staff—accommodations that were designed to seat comfortably approximately 800 readers and to afford work space for a hundred or so staff members in conditions that would conserve strength and encourage a corresponding quality in effort.

But the heart of the Library was, of course, the general bookstack—a ten deck tower extending downward in the central block of the northern side. This was a complete and compact unit formed of rock-based foundations, concrete floors, and a forest of steel supports. This bookstack and supplementary shelving in various rooms in other parts of the building afforded a total shelf space for some 600,000 volumes. Of course, when there is an expansive classification into which additions are inserted according to subject, any figure giving total shelf space is misleading, since some allowance of empty shelves scattered throughout the bookstack is essential for effective operation. It was therefore recognized that a capacity figure for workable conditions would prove to be not over 500,000 volumes. It should be added that the need which Dean Metcalf had been among the first to recognize, namely, that the University supply research facilities for graduate students, faculty, and visiting scholars, was in this new building met not only by the studies and seminars on the fifth floor, and by the accommodations of the Rare Book and Manuscript Division, but also by one hundred carrels or cubicles lining the northern side of the general bookstack.

Economy had been stressed in the making of the plans; and as it turned out, the date of erection was favorable for building costs. About 1938 prices began to be yeasty, and it has been estimated that by 1950 the expense of erection would have doubled. One effect of that economy was that when the moving had been completed, all parts of the new building were occupied. This absence of uncharted spaces had the result of shortening the interval until further expansion would be necessary. It had also not been sufficiently realized how stimulating to users of the Library and to donors of materials this impressive structure would prove; and what seemed to be a generous allowance for growth proved in some facilities to have been sadly underestimated. By 1944, when the Faculty Library Committee again found it necessary to concentrate on building plans, on the details for the addition to the northward, the pressure for more stack space, for more studies and carrels, for more special rooms had again become urgent. Hence, at the end of the first quarter of the University Library's second hundred years, the building problem was again a serious one. But by that time there was a clearer conception of what a library of university caliber involved and of its value to the University and to the whole region.

By 1950 there had also been a gain in housing and equipment for most of the department, school, and special collections. The Chemistry, Fine Arts, and Physics Libraries had acquired additional shelf space, the collections for the Institute for Research in the Social Sciences and for Rural Social Economics had been transferred to more spacious quarters in Minor Hall, and an attractive Nurses' Library had been opened in one of the medical buildings. The books of the music and public administration collections had for the most part been transferred to the Alderman Library, leaving a total of nine school and special collections. The three department libraries, Engineering, Law, and Medical, were in this period all moved into specially designed library sections of new buildings: the Engineering Library into Thornton Hall, occupied in 1936, the Law Library into Clark Hall, occupied in 1932, and the Medical Library into the medical group which was occupied in 1929. By 1950 hopes were immediate for further accommodations for the rapidly growing law collections, and the needs were patent for similar expansion of the engineering and medical collections. Thus in buildings and equipment the advance on the path of progress, for the general library and for a majority of the separate collections, had been greater during this period than during the entire preceding century.

4. THE CATALOGUE

The new general library building was the first essential for the reorganization of the library service. Essential also was an adequate catalogue of the printed books. This was no new problem. Of the list which Thomas Jefferson prepared in 1825 for the use of bookdealer Hilliard, we have earlier stated that by all counts it was a remarkable achievement. That statement has been reiterated through the course of this history like a musical theme; and it emerges once more at this point. To Hilliard the Jefferson achievement was an order list. To the University its greatest value was as a comprehensive and authoritative selection of the essential works in all fields of learning. To the Library it served as a model for the printed catalogue of 1828. That catalogue followed the list in the arrangement by subjects according to the Bacon-Jefferson system of classification. It

145

was thus virtually a shelf list. So also was William Wertenbaker's remarkable memory. The compiler of the 1828 catalogue and a wholehearted admirer of the Founder, he loyally kept that classification in use by shelving new books according to its subjects. In the 1850's Librarian Holcombe's two folio volume author catalogue entered books according to the Gildersleeve rules revised by the Visitors. Those rules, however, affected changes in cataloguing entry, not in classification. A succession of Librarians of brief terms and consequently short memories immediately followed Wertenbaker's retirement, and the cataloguing problem again became acute. The concern now was not for classification but for some form of cataloguing that would serve as a finding list. Adherence to the Bacon-Jefferson classification had been dying of inanition, and it expired unnoticed with the destruction of a large part of the original collection in the burning of the Rotunda. It is significant that Librarian Patton's adoption of the Dewey Decimal Classification is not even noted in the records.

Meantime some bibliothecal Eli Whitney had advocated use of a three by five library card (it is diverting to imagine Mr. Jefferson's possible reactions), and in the decades following, library cataloguing was thereby to expand mightily in usefulness—and in problems. In the consideration of what was to be placed on the fair surfaces of the library cards, the movement was to be from simplicity to elaborateness to an involved attempt to achieve maximum utility with minimum cost.

The use of cards at the University of Virginia Library had started before the date of the Rotunda fire, so that the cataloguing of the new, postfire collections was uniform in that respect. In other respects it was not so uniform. The earlier cataloguing illustrated the stage of simplicity—some of it had been very simple indeed. As later entries grew more elaborate, the contrast became glaring. By the beginning of the Library's second century, Librarian Patton was inaugurating a modest project of recataloguing; and his successor therefore had the advantage of being able to coordinate the new efforts with a process already under way. He also had the great advantage of the enthusiasm, unaccountable to many people, with which the little group of Cataloguers faced their intricate tasks.

By this time, however, the idea of developing a research as well as a college library was taking firm root. This of course rendered desirable an arrangement of the books that would facilitate the quests of graduate students and research scholars who would have direct access to the shelves. To this end, a subcommittee of the Faculty Library Committee, Chairman Metcalf, Professor Dumas Malone, and the Librarian being members, made a study of classification schemes. That subcommittee recommended the adoption of the Library of Congress classification. The recommendation was approved by the whole committee—but with the proviso that the change await favorable circumstances.

When that action was taken, in February 1929, the circumstances could scarcely have been less favorable. The Cataloguing Staff was small, the shelves at the Rotunda were overcrowded with books, there were no special funds, and no depository set of Library of Congress cards was available. Moreover this meant all of the library books, and it meant that until the change could be actually begun, all of the present cataloguing would afterwards have to be revised. It was a decision that required courage and a large draft on the reserves of patience.

Encouragement came soon through several favorable turns of fortune. Word was received that the Library at Princeton University had discarded a set of proof sheets of Library of Congress cards, arranged by subject. Princeton's Librarian, James Thayer Gerould, generously presented that set to the Library at the Rotunda. Herbert Put-

147

nam, Librarian of Congress, being apprised of the effort at Charlottesville, with like generosity donated all cards printed at the Library of Congress before the distribution of proof sheets had been started. Subscription to proof sheets following the Princeton set came within the means of the University of Virginia Library. The combination of the three sources afforded well nigh a complete set of Library of Congress cards, thus reducing time and expense in ordering cards for cataloguing, and at the same time supplying for research use a much needed bibliographical tool.

The interest manifested by the Library of Congress at the beginning continued in various effective ways throughout this cataloguing campaign. This is a type of service to which little publicity has been given. But the Library at the University of Virginia can join with many another Library in testimony that ultimate success in undertakings of this sort has depended to no small degree on the cooperation freely granted by the National Library in Washington.

Almost at the moment the decision was reached for adoption, whenever the time should be deemed propitious, of the Library of Congress classification, there was announcement of a grant to the University of Virginia from the General Education Board of a Humanities Fund for the five sessions from 1930 to 1935. A portion of that fund was allotted to the Library. This meant a real beginning in collection building on a research basis; and several Professors who were added to the Faculty by means of that fund were drawn into collaboration in the ensuing book selection. At once the proposition was strongly advanced that if the new books were to be made speedily available, the cost of processing them should be added to the purchase cost; in other words, that a part of the Library's share in that grant should be devoted to salaries for additional Cataloguers. The acceptance of the proposition was of strategic value then and later towards the solution of the inherited cataloguing problem.

Advantage was taken of the resultant enlargement of the Cataloguing Staff to segregate a small group for special cataloguing or for recataloguing projects. The removal in 1929 of the Medical Library from one of the oval rooms on the ground floor of the Rotunda to the new medical buildings at "The Corner" left that room available for this special Cataloguing Staff; and the medical collection itself was the first unit to be handled. That and the collection on Fine Arts, which had recently been located in Fayerweather Hall, occupied the special staff until September 1931. Work was then started on the Classical Library in Cabell Hall. The work on that unit, completed in July 1933, was a striking proof of the validity of the proposition that purchase and cataloguing costs should be linked; for some of the Hertz books acquired in 1895 were now for the first time made generally available.

It should be remembered, however, that all cataloguing was still under the divisions and symbols of the Dewey System. It was not until 1933, four years after the decision by the Faculty Library Committee, that a possible break appeared in the confining wall of circumstances. That came in the announcement one morning of a donation by William Andrews Clark of funds for a new building for the Department of Law, a building in which there should be more spacious equipment for the Law Library. Within a half hour after the announcement, request had been made for the use, until the new general library building should be secured and made ready, of the Law Library's vacated space and former equipment in Minor Hall. To Minor Hall, therefore, was moved the small special staff, to it were transferred some of the uncatalogued gift collections, and the strategy of a "nucleus library" was devised—a unit catalogued in the Library of Congress classification to become a nucleus for use in the hoped-for new building. It was pleasantly appropriate that the first gift collection to be handled was the private library of President Alderman, which had been donated by Mrs. Alderman.

Work on the nucleus library began in July 1933. It was interrupted by the cataloguing of the Lomb books on Optics, which were acquired in 1934, and of the books of the Engineering Library during their transfer in 1934-1935 from the Mechanical Laboratory to Thornton Hall, the new headquarters of the Department of Engineering. When the time came in 1938 for the Minor Hall group to move to the Alderman Library a total of 33,972 volumes had been catalogued, of which 24,788 were in the nucleus collection.

As soon as the new building was assured, it was estimated that February 1937 was the earliest possible date for the Cataloguers at the Rotunda to make their beginning in the use of the Library of Congress classification. Thereafter both groups of Cataloguers speeded their efforts; and at the end of the session of 1937-1938 there were altogether 76,853 volumes in the new catalogue. It was a pursuit race, however. For by that time the 131,422 total of 1925 had been increased to 303,502, and the magnitude of a cataloguing campaign on two fronts, backward and forward, had become impressively evident. So also had the value of that campaign. For with the new catalogue and the old filed side by side in the entrance hall of the Alderman building, one growing rapidly and the other more slowly shrinking in size, it was soon observed that the use by readers was being concentrated well nigh exclusively on the new.

This use by readers was given its rightful importance in the cataloguing campaign. Cataloguers, intent on their task, run some danger of coming to regard the catalogue as an end in itself, rather than a means for the service of users. Now it had so happened that the majority of the leaders in this undertaking at the University of Virginia had personally had experience in circulation work before becoming Cataloguers. Moreover, during the strenuous first years in the Alderman Library, when the Reference Division was sorely undermanned, it became the practice that volunteers from the Preparations Division should spend several hours weekly in reference service routines. Therefore, along with realization of the necessity of consistent maintenance of standards, there was kept active some recognition of the practical difficulties of a public unacquainted with cataloguing rules.

Ever since the readings in 1927 and 1928 from the American Library Association's *Survey of Libraries in the United States,* these Cataloguers had endeavored to keep abreast of general progress in cataloguing procedures, had taken part in library conferences and in such experiments as cooperative cataloguing, and had shared in the heart searching after the publication in the October 1941 issue of the *Library Quarterly* of Andrew Delbridge Osborn's "The Crisis in Cataloguing." During the years of the second world war, the University of Virginia Library had the gratification of renewing its earlier link with the Library of Congress, based on Thomas Jefferson's part in the founding of both libraries, by supplying safety storage for various valuable materials from the National Library and by housing its Union Catalogue, with its Staff. The resulting period of direct access to the Union Catalogue, that extraordinary asset to research, was of unique value to the University of Virginia Cataloguers. It was also a matter of local satisfaction that the University's cataloguing campaign enabled it to contribute to the National Union Catalogue copies of all its cards, including those of the Law Library. For that statement there should be clarification on two points.

The first looks back to an action by the Faculty Library Committee in 1928, establishing a policy of centralized library administration, to include all collections except the

Law Library. Prior to that action a study of another American Library Association publication, George Alan Works' *College and University Library Problems,* had proved useful. By that policy, matters of staff appointment, budget preparation, and book selection became the joint responsibility of the heads of the various departments or schools concerned and the Librarian or his representative; the acquisitions and preparations tasks were centered in the staff of the general library; the circulation procedures were performed by the staffs of the libraries in which the books were located; and reference aid was supplied by the local staffs or, when it seemed appropriate, by the reference staff of the general library. Since the cataloguing was done by the Preparations Division of the general library (with the public catalogue in the general library serving as a union catalogue for university books and with local catalogues at the separate libraries), it could become a standard order of business to supply cards to the National Union Catalogue.

As for the Law Library, that was benefiting immeasurably by the vigorous and constructive interest of the Law Alumni. In 1938 a special alumni committee, headed by Paul Brandon Barringer, Jr., prepared a detailed and searching report on the Law School with somewhat special reference to its Library. That and a survey made a year later by Elisha Riggs McConnell served as blueprints for reorganization of the Law Library. Its collections and its service became thereafter a focal point of concern for the Alumni of the Department of Law. It may indeed be noted that during the latter part of the 1925-1950 period, alumni interest in the Law, Medical, and Engineering Libraries and in the browsing room and international studies collections of the Alderman Library was in striking contrast to the widespread contention that the enthusiasm—or the criticism—of alumni is stimulated mainly by prowess on the playing fields.

Under this incitement from the Law Alumni, the reorganization of the Law Library was speeded in 1942 by the appointment of Miss Frances Farmer, a graduate in law and the former Law Librarian of the University of Richmond, to take charge of the cataloguing of the law collection. On the retirement of Mrs. Graves in 1945, with a noteworthy record of thirty-three years of service, Miss Farmer became Law Librarian. As in the case of the general library reorganization, some of the very difficulties of those years were turned to favorable account. For the severe drop in the enrollment of law students during war days resulted in minimum use of the law books and thereby speeded the progress of the cataloguing. By 1944 a survey of the results by Miles Oscar Price, Librarian of the Columbia University School of Law, brought forth a meed of hearty praise for the results—which had produced not only a notably effective catalogue for the Law Library in Clark Hall but also complete representation in the combined catalogue of university books in the Alderman Library and, with the approval of Dean Frederick Deane Goodwin Ribble and Miss Farmer, in the Union Catalogue at the Library of Congress. Therefore, because the cataloguing campaigns during 1925-1950 covered all the university books, the contribution of the University of Virginia to the National Union Catalogue was complete.

By the close—at least the fighting close—of the second world war, the termination of that huge cataloguing task was in sight. Some remnants remained, as did also the collection of public documents and an accumulation of pamphlets. But there was access to the documents by means of the symbols of the Superintendent of Documents; and pamphlet cataloguing, having run the gamut from an elaborate and costly method, had reached the stage of an experiment in simplified handling. Therefore the main business of cataloguing was thereafter reduced to the processing of current additions. The word "reduced" has reference to the vast undertaking that had been in operation. But there should be emphasis also on the fact that by 1950 the unending task of handling the yearly acquisitions had itself grown to major proportions. During the session of 1949-1950 the number of books made accessible for use in all of the University Libraries was 40,893. In the last year of Librarian Wertenbaker's active service, the total collection was reported as "about 36,000 volumes." Thus the increase in the single year 1949-1950 was considerably in excess of the whole collection at the end of its first fifty-five years. Moreover access to that earlier collection was not by the open sesame of a library card catalogue but by the tenacious but mortal memory of William Wertenbaker.

5. THE COLLECTIONS

That addition of 40,893 volumes during the last year of the 1925-1950 period is proof that in collection building also there had been progress. Thanks mainly to generosity on the part of faculty, alumni, and many friends of the University of Virginia, the progress had been continuous. It had increased in the later years—the presence of the new depository, secure and dignified, had undoubtedly given encouragement to donors. The recorded growth during the first five sessions of the period and during the last five sessions strikingly reveals this. The figures are of volumes made accessible, and include all of the university libraries. For the sessions from 1925 to 1930 they were 4,220, 3,858, 6,113, 8,773, 8,737; for the sessions from 1945 to 1950 they were 18,563, 23,135, 30,074, 36,597, and 40,893. It can readily be seen that any slackening of the cataloguing task as the over-all campaign grew to its close had been caught up by the increase in new acquisitions.

The University of Virginia's total of 131,422 volumes in

1925 had grown to a total of 592,390 in 1950. However, that 1950 figure by no means told the whole story. The figure was for complete and, for the most part, bound volumes. Such had been the method of computation maintained throughout the previous history of the Library. Had there been a change to the policy of enumeration by bibliographical units—a policy adopted by a number of university libraries during the last decade of the period—to that 1950 total there could have been added 243,404 unbound public documents, thousands of volumes of unbound periodicals and newspapers, and thousands of items of printed matter in a microfilm collection which by 1950 comprised 1,553 reels.

Moreover, those figures were for printed matter. But coincident with the emphasis on the research character of the Library, there had been expansion in the range of the collecting activities. In 1925 there was no record of photographs, pictures, and prints. But by 1950 the University Library had an available collection of 51,376 items. In 1925 there was also no record of maps. But by 1950 the total of separate maps had reached 73,098. It will be recalled that as early as 1825 the University had acquired the Lee Papers. Occasional manuscripts were received and preserved thereafter, until a census taken in 1929 revealed a total of 2,177 pieces. By July 1950 the total had mounted to the extraordinary figure of 3,504,100 pieces. Anyone attempting a graph of the growth of the manuscript collection would run the danger of a sudden loss of equilibrium.

The source of the non-book materials had almost exclusively been gifts. As for the purchase of books, in the state appropriations there had been a notable change from the penury of 1925. Both President Newcomb and President Darden had realized that special efforts were necessary in order to regain the ground lost during the prolonged periods of lean years that had characterized the first century and had given earnest support to library requests for appropriation advances, whenever such requests seemed soundly conceived. But it had been necessary that library advances proceed along several lines, with the result that the rate of increase in the state appropriations for books, periodicals, and binding had not kept abreast of the rate of increase for other expenses.

There were valid reasons for the difference in emphasis. One of the benefits from the Humanities Fund of 1930-1935 had been the demonstration that a part of the cost of library books is hidden in the salary expenses for the dozen or more processing procedures. The successful operation of the cataloguing campaign had made expansion of the Preparations Division necessary. As for the new building, it had not been a charge against the State, but its servicing had required a considerable increase in several Divisions of the Staff. So also had the extension of the hours of opening to ninety-eight a week, in response to demands from students and faculty that bore gratifying testimony to the Library's usefulness. The State Personnel Act of 1942 had affected all Library Staffs and Divisions, and had corrected some long-standing inequalities in salary; and alert consideration by the General Assembly of Virginia of "white collar" difficulties in a period of devaluation of the purchasing power of the dollar had resulted, in the closing years of this period, in compensating adjustments upward in the stipends of the employees. Therefore advances in the total appropriations to the University Library had been to a large degree the result, partly planned and partly automatic, of higher salaries paid to a larger staff.

However, there had not been, to any appreciable degree, compensatory adjustments upward in purchase funds to meet the greatly increased costs of books, periodicals, and binding. Moreover, such state advances as there had been had barely kept pace with the large postwar growth in enrollment, and the advances had therefore been largely absorbed by college library needs, by the support of undergraduate curriculum courses. For the means to develop the University Library as a research center, it had therefore been necessary to depend on gifts from outside.

To legislators struggling with the complexities of the operating budgets of a modern State, the term "research" was liable to seem vague and intangible, especially if it be research in the realm of the humanities and social sciences. Even for scientific research there was a disposition to let that be a charge on the Federal Government—it would appear that the arguments for States' Rights were urged with somewhat less enthusiasm at that point. Consequently, for the Library of a State University there was likely to be the complication of having to prove definite values without the means to create the values—to make bricks without straw.

Yet there were appearing, though dimly as yet, occasional signs of a quickening realization that great issues were involved in the effort to increase and to extend knowledge, not only in sciences, but also in the social sciences, in the humanities, in religion. There is a saying attributed to President Alderman, that liberty is not an heritage but a fresh conquest for each generation. For the generation following the second world war this appeared to be taking the dread form of a conquest of fear. There were mounting attacks upon human liberty, from one direction formidable because of their might, from another direction frightening because of their subtlety. Even the means to oppose them were weighted with the possibility of annihilation of both foe and friend. In the face of such a crisis there were the most vital reasons for the mobilization of every incentive to a humane and sanely balanced way of life. Therefore the State of Virginia as well as its University had reason for gratitude to the generosity that had made possible the beginnings and the expansion of research services by the University Library. It had not been a mere flight of fancy that had inspired President Alderman's appraisal of the Library in his last words to a university audience: "The very angels in heaven might well envy men and women who have the power and the desire *to set free the forces that inhere in this intention.*"

It is impracticable within the compass of this history to name the thousands of men and women who responded during these years 1925 to 1950. In view of the extended notice that has been given to individual gifts made during the years immediately following the Rotunda fire, the omission of a similarly full record opens this section of the library story to the charge of a grave deficiency, of well-nigh invidious neglect of the new host of benefactors. It was a host. The gifts of money for the purchase of books and manuscripts were in these twenty-five years nearly five times the total for the whole hundred years preceding; and the gifts of books and manuscripts were at an even greater ratio of increase.

But the difficulty of including individual recognition in this historical record was largely overcome in the Library itself. The practice had been adopted of using gift book-plates, a number of them specially designed, for books donated or for books purchased on donated funds. There had been some attempt to extend the practice backward, to include books known to have been donated in earlier years. Thus the casual reader might discover that the book he had chanced to open had once been a personal possession of President Alderman or of President Newcomb, of Professor Charles William Kent or of Professor John B. Minor, of Bishop Collins Denny or of Walter Hines Page; or that the book had been acquired from funds in memory of Elizabeth Cocke Coles or of Dean Metcalf or of Peters Rushton— or of one of the heroic students who had in the second world war sacrificed his life for his country's freedom and for the freedom of mankind.

> They shall grow not old, as we that are left grow old;
> Age shall not weary them, nor the years condemn.
> At the going down of the sun and in the morning
> We will remember them.

Thus in the Library itself this storehouse of books became a storehouse of associations of affection and gratitude. The removal from the Rotunda had not made so severe a break with the past as some had feared that it would. Indeed, in the bookplates, and in the McGregor and Garnett and Taylor Rooms, and in many other ways, there had flooded in new and even deeper associations. In the rare book section there was a modest but substantial bookcase filled with the carefully preserved college books which Robert Carter Berkeley had used during his student days between 1857 and 1861. There was the family collection assembled by Joseph Carrington Cabell, who had been closely associated with Jefferson in the founding of the University, and by his nephew, Nathaniel Francis Cabell. And there was the Garnett home library, which had remained undisturbed at "Elmwood" in Essex County, Virginia, from the death of Muscoe Russell Hunter Garnett in 1864 until it was moved intact in 1938 into an appropriately furnished room in the Alderman Library. There can be few existing examples as complete as this was of the reading background of a leading Virginia family in the days before the war of 1861-1865. This had also a special link with the history of the University of Virginia Library, since its owner, Muscoe Garnett, a graduate of both the College and the Department of Law, had been Chairman of that very active Library Committee of the Board of Visitors in the prosperous 1850's. There were intimations, indeed, that with the Garnett books had come even more unusual associations. For to staff members, voluntarily devoting midnight hours to the crowding tasks of that period, came fleeting suspicions that the gentle guest of "Elmwood," who had for long years performed grateful returns for hospitality by the ghostly caretaking of the books of his whilom host, had foregathered for congenial whisperings and comradely excursions in the halls of the new building with the book-loving spirit of Bennett Wood Green, which had formerly been wont to make its nightly rounds through the galleries of the Rotunda. Here were research possibilities in the elusive subject of the transplanting of ghosts.

But thanks to the donations received during these years, there were research possibilities more tangible at midday. Though the many donors of useful and attractive and valuable *general* collections must go unnamed in this 1925-1950 record, there can be mention of some of those whose gifts of books or money have had importance in supplying research material in *special* subjects. It is recognized that such discrimination among donors is unfortunate and unfair—and this is deeply regretted. Yet this risk has been taken in order that there may be indication of the areas in which research possibilities had by 1950 developed in this University Library.

Naturally the collection of photographs, pictures, and prints became a rich mine for local history and for the history of the University of Virginia. An acquisition of special university interest, presented by William Hillman Wranek, Jr., was the University Press Bureau's accumulation of photographs, and also newspaper clippings and press releases, covering this whole period, 1925 to 1950. An intriguing commentary on state and national subjects of social and political content during the same period was furnished by the gift by the artist of the originals of the Fred O. Seibel cartoons featured in the *Richmond Times Dispatch*. An extensive collection of striking British war posters of the second world war had been contributed by Edward Reilly

Stettinius, Jr., Lend-Lease Administrator and later Secretary of State. A donation of outstanding value had been the bequest by T. Catesby Jones of his collection of modern French prints. It was with a display from those prints that a new exhibition gallery in the passage between the entrances to the McGregor Room and the Acquisitions Division had been formally opened in 1949.

The map collection was likewise of research importance, starting with Virginia and featuring such early examples as the work of Peter Jefferson, Thomas Jefferson's father; reaching to other States, as in the Kentucky collection assembled by John Calvin Doolan; and extending both backward and outward because of the interest of Tracy W. McGregor in cosmography and early geography. The rapid growth of the map collection after the second world war had been greatly aided by the designation of the University of Virginia Library as a depository of the Army Map Service.

That at the beginning of this period the concept of a research library had not reached the stage of specific planning and action was evident in the conventional, not to say apathetic, attitude towards manuscripts and rare books. So far as manuscripts were concerned, the change of attitude was stimulated by examples of activity in neighboring States and by outside criticisms of the comparative lethargy at the University of Virginia. The impulses to progress are various. Sometimes irritation is a potent persuader. It would seem to be a fair statement concerning the start at this time of an active programme of manuscript collecting that several forces met in harmonious conjunction; and that the initiative once seized was retained by consistent and untiring effort.

The initial move towards systematic collection of manuscripts was the preparation and distribution by first class mail early in 1930 of 20,000 copies of a broadside written by Professor Thornton. That this was regarded as important was made clear by the selection of William Mynn Thornton as its composer; and that it had the official support of the University was emphasized by the display of six signatures: of the President of the University, of the Rector of the Board of Visitors, of Professor Thornton, of the senior Professsor of History, of the Chairman of the Faculty Library Committee, and of the Librarian. The document earnestly called attention to the widespread destruction of Virginia's manuscript memorials of her past—destruction by "the devastations of war, the conflagrations of ancient homes, the besom of the tidy housewife, and the backyard bonfire." It announced that the University of Virginia was now prepared to offer its aid "in the preservation, the study, the interpretation, and the publication of the memorials of Virginia's social, industrial, political, and intellectual life."

Something like this had been implicit in Jefferson's own interests and activities in 1825; and this pronouncement of 1930 bears interesting comparison with the magisterial manifesto prepared by Professor Holmes in 1861. But this time means for actual fulfillment were secured by the appointment in 1930 of an Archivist as a library official; and there was the good fortune that a trained historian eminently fitted for the new position was available. Dr. Lester J. Cappon had been Research Associate in History in the University's Institute for Research in the Social Sciences, and had just completed, as a monograph of that Institute, a 900 page *Bibliography of Virginia History since 1865*. Through the interest of the American Council of Learned Societies in this archival project, a grant was secured from the Carnegie Corporation for the initiation of the project; this was followed by effective assistance from Professor Gee, the Director of this Research Institute at the University of Virginia.

This archival project was fortunate also in its timing. The years between the first and second world wars had seen the emergence of a new viewpoint in historical research, in which economic and social planning had become central. Involved in the movement had been such organizations as the American Council of Learned Societies, the Social Science Research Council, the Public Archives Commission of the American Historical Association, the Public Documents Committee of the American Library Association, and national and state archives commissions. Developing directly out of the movement were such organizations as the Society of American Archivists and the American Association for State and Local History—in both of which Doctor Cappon was to hold official positions. And coincident with the movement came rapid advances in microphotography. Moreover the movement proved to have the stamina and flexibility requisite for adaptation to world-wide warfare and economic depression.

The wording of the Thornton broadside had fitted admirably into this national movement. Much more than the collecting of manuscripts was involved. The full intent of the University of Virginia project became revealed as the programme for the Archivist came into operation. The central purpose was to facilitate and encourage research—to do the spade work, as it were, for historical scholarship. Priority was to be given to a survey of the historical materials existing in Virginia, which would serve as a guide to research workers; accessibility was to be emphasized, as well as preservation; and the principle of cooperation with other agencies was to be upheld as a definite policy. As in the national movement, the scope of the undertaking was to be broadened by interpreting historical materials as including every record bearing on human relationships.

In the method proposed for carrying out this programme there was something of novelty. The plan involved careful, on-the-spot examination of the material in each of the State's one hundred counties. By 1935 twenty-seven counties had been surveyed. But in that year the Historical Records Survey, an offspring of the depression, had undertaken a similar county by county examination for the whole country and had thus rendered further effort of this sort in the University of Virginia undertaking unnecessary. However, the administrators of the national survey looked to Doctor Cappon, as a pioneer in such a project, for counsel and for the initial direction of their efforts in Virginia. Again when the ominous signs of an approaching second world war turned the attention of the new archival movement to the collection of war materials, Doctor Cappon was called upon to review the efforts for such collection which had been made during the first world war and to prepare a manual for systematic procedures during the progress of the coming conflict. The University of Virginia had in 1925 seemed pathetically behind it its work with manuscripts. But when the awakening came, in 1930, it was well timed. For a decade later, out of the University of Virginia were coming both example and leadership.

Doctor Cappon continued as Archivist until 1945, when he was called to another new position, that of Research Editor for the Institute of Early American History and Culture in Williamsburg, Virginia. He was, however, retained on the roll of the University of Virginia Library as Honorary Consultant in Archives—and the policy of cooperation was thereafter emphasized by the friendly bonds between the Williamsburg Institute and the University Library. Like the Librarian, Doctor Cappon had not been a graduate of the University of Virginia, his training having been received at the University of Wisconsin and Harvard University. But by 1945 there was a University of Virginia alumnus, Francis Lewis Berkeley, Jr., who to a marked degree had the desired background, the keen interest and untiring energy, and the flair for uncovering manuscript caches that made him an ideal successor in this library archival position.

The actual collecting of manuscripts had thus been linked with broader plans for service to historical scholarship. The response to the Thornton broadside had, however, been immediate and extensive; and later, when it became known that the new library building afforded safety to an unusual degree, the inflow of manuscripts notably increased. The survey of the counties also had resulted in the decision by many private owners of papers to place them for safekeeping, either as gifts or as deposits, in the University of Virginia Library. Althogether this effort at the University met with loyal and widespread support. It was almost exclusively a gift collection. All of the possibilities listed by Professor Thornton—"in the garrets and cellars and closets of old houses, in ancient mills and storerooms and barns, on dusty book shelves, and in discarded trunks"—all these had proved to be actual sources of manuscript material. There were also a few cases where valuable items had been purchased—by Clifton Waller Barrett, by William Andrews Clark, by William Sobieski Hildreth, by Robert Coleman Taylor, as examples—and presented to the University Library; and in certain other cases contributions of money had been made—by Robert Hill Carter, Joseph Manuel Hartfield, Thomas Catesby Jones, Cazenove Gardner Lee, as examples—in order that special and much desired items could be acquired by purchase. The items thus purchased formed but a small portion of the whole manuscript collection, but they ranked high in research value.

As covering all forms of human relationship, the range of subjects was wide. But the geographical area was chiefly Virginia and the southeastern States. From the beginning the official archives of the University had constituted an important division of the manuscript holdings. The earliest minutes of the meetings of the Board of Visitors were in Jefferson's own handwriting; and those immediately following carried the autograph signatures of Jefferson and Madison and Monroe, of Joseph Carrington Cabell and John Hartwell Cocke. For each of those founders there were also individual collections of letters and papers, the Jefferson collection at the University Library numbering by 1950 well over 2,000 pieces.

In the general political field, the manuscript collection contained papers of a number of European statesmen and their colonial deputies, of leading figures of the Revolutionary period, of the foremost Southern participants in the establishment of the new nation, and of a large company of Virginians who through the history of this Commonwealth had made individual contributions in the service of the State and Nation. In the literary field there were letters and manuscripts not only of Southern writers, but also of a rather wide range of American and English authors. More local were the educational and philanthropic and church records, but those contained much matter pertinent to social studies; as did also a collection of considerable size of business records. Family papers had been received by gift and deposit from over three hundred families, though by common consent genealogical research continued to be centered in the Virginia State Library and in the Library of the Virginia Historical Society in Richmond.

The effort to make all this material available as rapidly as possible had placed a tremendous and exacting task upon the Staff of the Rare Book and Manuscript Division, since for manuscripts that Staff had to perform much of the acquisition and all of the preparation processes as well as the reference work for scholarly users. There had been, however, exciting moments injected into the long hours of processing, as when letters located in one collection were found to be replies to letters located in another collection. A hint of what was involved in this manuscript programme may be given by reference to the records of the Low Moor Iron Company, which were acquired in 1939. That business collection covered the complete history of a company located near Clifton Forge in Alleghany County, Virginia, from its founding in 1873 until it ceased operations in 1930. The records on arrival at the Library were found to weigh approximately twelve tons. As soon as the processing procedures could be got under way, there was assurance that the material was of service for a study then current of the southern iron industry. There were also incidental discoveries, of a letter written by Calvin Coolidge in 1900, when he was practicing law in Northampton, Massachusetts, and of a letter written by Franklin D. Roosevelt in 1918, while he was Assistant Secretary of the Navy; and with regard to a Connecticut-born mining engineer, William Sumner Hungerford, who was for a time superintendent of the Low Moor Iron Works, an interesting biographical sketch in manuscript, written by his daughter, was found in a collection acquired from an entirely different source.

For rare books also the beginning was with Virginia. In 1929 the southeastern wing of the Rotunda buildings became available for library use, and it was reserved for the books and manuscripts of a special Virginia Collection. Miss Frances Elizabeth Harshbarger, who had been a graduate student in History, was in charge until 1934, when she left to become Mrs. Joseph Lee Kinzie. Under her successor, John Cook Wyllie, to the Virginia Collection were gradually added other rare books and manuscripts; and during the year following the removal to the Alderman Library building, the Herculean task was performed of searching out and separating the rare books from the whole book collection. In that same year were acquired the McGregor Library and the Edward L. Stone collection, the latter

167

illustrative of the history of bookmaking; and to the University Library there had in reality been added the active services of a research center.

The addition of the McGregor Library was a highly important factor in the research developments at the University of Virginia. This collection came to a small library at the moment when that library was attempting a new role. The significance of the collection was therefore much greater than it would have been in a library rich in such collections, or in a library not committed to an ambitious programme. Moreover the conditions of the gift to a notable degree ensured its continued vitality. Altogether, this proved to be an outstanding example of constructive benefaction.

The collection had been assembled by the late Tracy W. McGregor of Detroit, a man aptly described by his friend, Judge Henry Schoolcraft Hulbert, as "a quiet, unassuming Christian gentleman with high spiritual attributes and a great civic conscience." One of the recognized book collectors of his day, his private library reflected the interests of a practical humanist concerned with freeing the spirit of mankind and widening the boundaries of endeavor. Limiting the field largely to material in the English language, he specialized in English and American literature and, more particularly, in American history. At his death his library was left to the Trustees of McGregor Fund, a foundation established in 1925 for the administration of charitable and educational undertakings that would be in accord with the spirit of his own endeavor. Carrying out what they felt to have been his intention, the trustees, headed by Judge Hulbert, presented the library to the University of Virginia and, as an appropriate memorial, equipped and furnished a portion of the rare book section in the new building as a gentleman's library room. This rare book collection of some 5,000 volumes (a more general collection of fully 12,500 volumes was also presented) afforded basic reason for extension of the Faculty and of the graduate work in American history; the annual contribution of $7,500 for the purchase of new material (which sum, by agreement, was supplemented by the University to ensure a total of $10,000 a year) was a guarantee of healthy growth; and the establishment of an Advisory Committee, on which the Trustees of McGregor Fund would be represented, gave promise of their continued interest and friendly counsel—a promise that happily attained unqualified fulfillment.

To the McGregor Fund, thus annually available, and to the income from the Byrd Fund, was in 1939 added the income from a fund established in memory of Elizabeth Cocke Coles by a bequest from Walter Derossett Coles. The McGregor Fund was for American History (with occasional use for English and American Literature) and the Byrd and Coles Funds were for the purchase of Virginiana. Following a plan suggested by Dr. Thomas Perkins Abernethy, Professor of American History, the selection of the books and manuscripts was performed by a group composed of the three Professors of American History, the Librarian, and the heads of the library divisions directly concerned. This group met fortnightly during the session, and was thus able to combine long time planning with immediate action whenever special opportunities for acquisition emerged.

With books and manuscripts and other materials combined, the research strength of the University of Virginia Library was by 1950 outstanding for the political and social history of the southeastern section of the United States. This field included the material on the Negro acquired through the opportunity offered by the James Fund, which had been supplemented in 1925, 1928, and 1937. During this period there were gains also in other fields of history.

The gatherings from two decades of research by the late Raymond Gorges on the annals of the Gorges family brought in 1943 unique material on the colonial history of Maine. Books and funds donated by an alert and loyal alumnus, Harcourt Parrish, broadened the possibilities of study of Poland and of South America. A library-minded foreign service officer of the State Department, Robert Smith Simpson, effectively recorded the successive posts in his diplomatic career by donating extensive assemblage of material on Belgium, Greece, and Mexico. A memorial fund to an aviator hero of the second world war, William Wylie Morton, extended helpfully the acquisition of books on Russia. The initial stimulus toward the establishment of the Woodrow Wilson School of Foreign Affairs at the University of Virginia was the enthusiastic response of the Alumni to the promotion by Branch Spalding of a plan for an International Studies Fund. The income from that fund was later supplemented by grants from the Jesse Jones Fund which was in 1945 donated to the Woodrow Wilson School.

The McGregor Library texts from the early geographers and explorers have been mentioned in connection with the map collection. These were supplemented in 1943 by a set of fifty-five volumes of the writings of Henry Harrisse, donated by Albert Ulman Walter, alumnus of the University and relative of the French bibliographer and historian. In general collections, such as those donated by Barnard Shipp in 1903 and by William Elliott Dold in 1936, had been found considerable material on geography and travel; and the resulting accumulation in that field proved gratifyingly serviceable for the wartime use by the School of Military Government, which held its successive sessions at the University of Virginia, and by the School of Geography, which was a postwar development in connection with the Woodrow Wilson School of Foreign Affairs. At the close of the period there were being received from Dr. and Mrs.

Edward Smith Craighill Handy the beginnings of a "Far Places Collection" which bade fair to be of both research and popular interest, and from Mrs. Thomas Ellett the extensive collection of her father, Colonel John Bigelow, on the discovery of the New World and on waterways, with emphasis on the Suez and Panama Canals.

In the subjects of Political Science and of Economics, including Rural Social Economics, the acquisition of material on a graduate study level had been facilitated by grants from the General Education Board during the years from 1937 to 1943. Political Science had been aided also by books from the private libraries of Henry Harford Cumming, Jr., and Bruce Williams, both of whom had been members of the Faculty of Political Science at the University of Virginia, and from the library of William Franklin Willoughby, Director of the Institute for Government Research in Washington. Economics had also profited from a book fund raised by student enterprise during the years from 1929 to 1947.

Reference has earlier been made to the aid rendered in book selection during this period by the faculty members chosen by the Schools and Departments to act in liaison with the Library, both for approval of current requests and for long time planning. Among those outstanding for such services were Duncan Clark Hyde, Professor of Economics, and Albert George Adam Balz, Corcoran Professor of Philosophy. Gifts to Philosophy had been moderate in amount, including endowment funds established by James Reese McKeldin in 1925 and by Professor Balz in 1950 and books coming from the private library of Professor Albert Lefevre in 1929. But the planned programme, though having to proceed slowly, was producing research possibilities by the end of this period.

In the general field of Language and Literature, the range by 1950 was from meagre holdings in Oriental subjects to collections of distinction in English and American Literature. There has already been mention of the donations of literary manuscripts. Gifts of money and of books had also been received. Memorial funds had been contributed for John Calvin Metcalf, long time Chairman of the Faculty Library Committee, and for Urban Joseph Peters Rushton, whose inspiring services as teacher and administrator had been terminated by his untimely death in 1949. Professor Rushton had himself, with characteristic impulses of gratitude and affection, created funds in memory of Asher Hinds, a former teacher of his at Princeton, and of Donald Randolph Reed, a student of his whose life had been lost during World War II. The Rushton gifts and the memorial to him emphasized the subject of Literary Criticism. Another Professor, Herman Patrick Johnson, had contributed money for the purchase of eighteenth century English works; and from an alumnus, Clifton Waller Barrett, whose generous gifts to the Library of his University carried the savor of his own sensitive appreciation of fineness in literature, had been coming, beginning in 1946, donations towards the acquisition of O. Henry material, and towards a Barrett literary manuscript collection. Meantime, throughout this period the Tunstall endowment for Poetry, established in 1919, had proved of continuing value. As for contributions of books, several had been outstanding. The Sadleir-Black collection in Gothic Fiction, presented by Robert Kerr Black in 1942 and supplemented later by him and by Linton Reynolds Massey, afforded exceptional opportunity for research in that tempting field. In addition to the Ingram material on Edgar Allan Poe acquired in 1921, Mr. Barrett had begun contributions to a Poe collection that would bring appropriate distinction to the Library of which the student Poe had made use. A choice group of T. S. Eliot items had been bequeathed in 1936 by another alumnus, David Schwab. The McGregor Library included valuable editions scattered through the whole field of English and American Literature; and so also had gifts from Clifton Waller Barrett, Samuel Merrifield Bemiss, William Andrews Clark, Mrs. Robert Coleman Taylor, and Henry Trautmann. Mrs. Taylor's collection, which, like the Garnett Library, was housed in a separate room, displayed the annals of American fiction. It consisted of several leading examples for each year from colonial times to the present.

In addition to its books and manuscripts, this Library had been one of a group of fourteen American libraries which in 1936 began subscription to microfilm reproductions of works printed in English or in England before 1550 —a cooperative project devised to ensure preservation and availability of research material. This project was later extended in scope; and its value was more acutely realized as the originals came under the dangers of the second world war bombing raids.

The grant by the General Education Board of the so-called Humanities Fund during the five sessions from 1930 to 1935 permitted systematic acquisition of material on a graduate study and research basis in English, Germanic, and Romance Philology and in Classical Archaeology, the congenial work of selection benefiting from the trained judgments of Professors Archibald Anderson Hill, Frederic Turnbull Wood, Earl Godfrey Mellor, Alexander David Fraser, and of Professor Joseph Médard Carrière, who joined the Faculty in 1942. Gifts of books in French had come from the private collections of Algernon Coleman, Professor at the University of Chicago, and of Richard Henry Wilson, who was Professor at the University of Virginia from 1899 to 1940; and in German from the working library of William Harrison Faulkner, who had served on the Faculty of the University of Virginia for an equally long term, from 1902 to 1944. In 1946 Mrs. Henry Waldo Greenough donated money for the purchase of books in

Italian. The favorable start towards new collections in Greek and Latin which acquisition of the Hertz and Price books had given shortly after the burning of the Rotunda was followed by a lean period. But after 1925 the classical holdings benefited from the bequest of his private library by William Gwathmey Manly, Professor of Latin at the University of Missouri, and by books on classical topics which had belonged to William Elisha Peters, Professor of Latin at the University of Virginia from 1865 to 1902. At the close of this 1925-1950 period, endowment funds in honor of Walter Alexander Montgomery, Professor of Latin, and of Robert Henning Webb, Professor of Greek, were about to become available. As for the material in Archaeology, carefully chosen by Professor Fraser in his use of the Humanities Fund, that had been supplemented in 1932 and 1944 by donations from David Randall-MacIver.

There had been a place for the study of Architecture in Jefferson's conception of the education needed for the youth of the new nation. In the erection of the buildings enclosing the central lawn he had achieved illustrations for such a course. But he got the pictures without the print, for it proved too early for this idea to be accepted. There is a hint, however, that his desire to have Architecture and Art included in the curriculum was well enough and favorably enough known to make it seem possible that there would be an early addition of a "School" in those subjects. When the Library's printed catalogue appeared in 1828, its first twenty-seven sections were all of subjects which would fit into the studies of the eight original "Schools." Into its twenty-ninth section, as a miscellany, were compressed Jefferson's original classification chapters thirty-one through forty-two—and the compilers would seem to have been justified if they deemed that the material in that miscellany would not for some time be likely to come within curriculum range. But immediately following the curriculum sections, one to twenty-seven, and immediately before the non-curriculum miscellany, section twenty-nine, was a section, twenty-eight, for Architecture, Designing, Painting, Sculpture, and Music. The forty-three titles, 102 volumes, of this section thus separated would on the library shelves be conveniently located together for use for a new School of Art and Architecture and Music.

As it turned out, this foresight was rather far sight. The charter for the University was granted in 1819. Exactly one hundred years later, in 1919, the creative interest of Paul Goodloe McIntire led to the establishment of Schools of Fine Arts and of Music, both of which were to bear this generous donor's name. The books in that twenty-eighth section had been lost in the flames; and by 1919 the general library was too cramped, both in space and in funds, to give more than casual support to the new "Schools." But by 1925 a start had been made, on equipment funds donated by Mr. McIntire, to form separate laboratory libraries for both Schools. A grant from the Carnegie Corporation in the session of 1927-1928 enabled Professors Edmund Schureman Campbell for Art and Architecture and Arthur Fickenscher for Music to add effective depth to the two collections. Research material had of course been sought in fine arts topics relating to Thomas Jefferson's own interests and achievements. Valuable additions were later made in special subjects; for example, by books donated by Thomas Catesby Jones to supplement his collection of French prints; and by the acquisition of the Alexander McKay Smith collection of Eighteenth Century Chamber Music. In fact by 1938 in the American Library Association publication *Resources of Southern Libraries,* edited by Robert Bingham Downs, it was stated that probably the best rounded collection of Musicology in the South was at the University of Virginia.

But if Mr. Jefferson a hundred years later would have

found the gathering of books in the Fine Arts to be proceed-
ing as he had planned, he would have been somewhat
puzzled by the gathering of books on Education as a separate subject. In the forty-two chapters of the final form of
his classification system there was none which bore the subject heading Education. When Jefferson wrote on that subject, he was considering education as a whole, not as one of
the parts. It is curious, though it is probably of no very
great significance, that the heading Education made an
appearance in that 1828 catalogue of the University of Virginia Library, printed two years after Jefferson's death—and
that it appeared in connection with that twenty-ninth miscellany section. For that polygenous section bore the title
"Miscellaneous, including Poetry, Rhetoric, Education,
&c." How had the student-librarian compiler (his major
subject of study was Law) and his two supervisors, the Professor of Mathematics and the Professor of Medicine, hit
upon that use of the word?

Altogether there were 393 titles listed in that Miscellany. Of those only four carried the word Education. One
was a copy, presented by the author, of a "Discourse on
Popular Education" delivered by Charles Fenton Mercer
before the American Whig and Cliosophic Societies at
Princeton University in September 1826, two months after
Jefferson's death. The other three were works in German.
Since in the 1828 catalogue all titles in foreign languages
were translated into English, a glance at the three German
originals reveals that the inclusion in each of some form of
the word *Erziehen* evidently led the compiler to enter "On
Education" as a convenient simplification of the whole
titles. As a matter of fact, none of the three was an educational treatise in the twentieth century manner. One may
venture the guess, therefore, that convenience was the
simple cause of this rather extreme case of synecdochism—
of using a word that had proved handy in the translation

of three titles for a whole section of 393 titles. Unlike Jefferson's proposition for a curriculum course in Architecture, this 1828 use of the term Education would appear to be of little historical significance.

Like Thomas Jefferson, President Alderman was a crusader for education. Their goals were the same, but there was some difference in technique. It was at the time of the inauguration of President Alderman in 1905 that the formation of the Curry Memorial School of Education was announced; and it was in 1920 after the death of the first Professor of Education, William Harry Heck, that the gift of his private library made possible the establishment of an Education Library. That excellent working collection continued to be the nucleus of the separate material on Education. In the next thirty years moderate growth was aided by donations of funds by Alfred William Erickson and by the educational fraternity Phi Delta Kappa. Gifts of material of research possibilities had come from James Gibson Johnson, long time Superintendent of the Charlottesville Public Schools, from Reaumur Coleman Stearnes, a former Superintendent of Public Instruction in Virginia, and from Joseph Dupuy Eggleston, who was in turn Virginia's Superintendent of Public Instruction, President of the Virginia Polytechnic Institute, and President of Hampden-Sydney College.

It will have been noted that the story of the Law Library has been one of a good measure of state and alumni support and of favorable fortune. That it had got off to an excellent start was revealed in the 1828 catalogue, the books in law numbering more than in any other single subject. In the later periods, when library appropriations from state funds were running dry, there had been usually at least a trickle for law books; and when the streams were filling up, as in the last decade of the 1925-1950 period, the alert law alumni were ready with effective measures for irrigation.

Moreover, the law collection alone has had an uninterrupted history, since it escaped destruction by the Rotunda fire. In 1925 the law collection contained over 20,000 volumes. Its increase in the next twenty-five years was more than fourfold, the total in 1950 being 88,635 volumes; and the indications were that a figure of six digits would soon be reached. Since a large proportion of the volumes in a law library is in series which report cases, the average importance of the volumes is more steady; and the total number of volumes is therefore likely to be a more accurate gauge of value that it is in the majority of subjects. On this basis and on the basis of the cataloguing campaign and of the expansion of the library services, the Law Library at the University of Virginia was in 1950 attaining a position of preeminence in the Southern States.

In connection with the law cataloguing campaign, it has been indicated that the Alumni had taken an active and effective part in planning as well as in donations. But in donations too the support was outstanding. In this period the Burdow, Dancy-Garth, and T. C. Smith endowment funds had been added, expendable funds had been received from alumni subscription, the estate of James Gordon Bohannon, the Memorial Welfare Association, H. Dent Minor, the Raleigh Colston Minor Memorial, the Sigma Nu Phi Fraternity, Robert Coleman Taylor, and the William Henry White lectureship—the last to be used for a collection on Constitutional Law. In this same period there had been gift acquisitions of books from the private collections of Judge Beverley Tucker Crump, John Shaw Field, Joseph Manuel Hartfield, William Jett Lauck, John Barbee and Raleigh Colston Minor, John Bassett Moore (as additions to his collection on International Law), Charles B. Samuels, and Judge George Curle Webb. There had also come by donation manuscript material from Justice James Clark McReynolds and from Judge John Munro Woolsey.

Law instruction had in this period been extended to include graduate studies and research, and for those purposes the law collection was proving to be favorably equipped.

The University of Virginia's books on Medicine, unlike its books on Law, had practically all been acquired after the Rotunda fire. By 1925, thirty years later, the Medical Library was described in the University Catalogue as containing "upwards of 7,000 volumes." But like the Law Library its increase in the next twenty-five years was more than fourfold. To be specific, the number of catalogued and available medical volumes in 1950 was 29,560. As an advantage from location in a University, there were also accessible to the medical faculty and students such university collections as those in Biology, Chemistry, and Psychology, and a considerable number of general medical books in the Alderman Library.

Several valuable donations of medical books came to the University of Virginia during this latest period; and for the first time, as far as the Medical Library was concerned, there were gifts of money, both in the form of endowments and of expendable funds. In 1930 the important medical library of the German physician, Dr. Adolf Richard Henle, was acquired through funds donated by the Department of Surgery and Gynecology. By gift came books from the private collections of William James Crittenden, Rudolf Wieser Holmes, Jefferson Randolph Kean, David Russell Lyman, and Marshall John Payne; and from an impressive number of members of the University Medical Faculty: John Staige Davis, James Carroll Flippin, William Hall Goodwin, Halstead Shipman Hedges, Theodore Hough, Kenneth Fuller Maxcy, Henry Bearden Mulholland, John Henry Neff, Lawrence Thomas Royster, Stephen Hurt Watts, and Richard Henry Whitehead. Doctor Watts's donation was notable for the number of rare medical texts that were included; and he also established

179

an endowment fund. Other endowment funds were received from William Evelyn Hopkins and from members of the family of Eugene Ezra Neff as a memorial to Doctor Neff. Beginning in 1937 the Medical Alumni, particularly those residing in the neighborhood of New York City, made generous annual contributions of funds. Other expendable funds came from Miss Addie Cintra Cox, William Dandridge Haden, Francis Henry McGovern, and Frederick Henry Wilke.

As has been earlier pointed out, systematic and persistent efforts had been producing gratifying results towards completing the runs of learned journals in the field of Chemistry and the runs of annual reports of observatories in the field of Astronomy. In Physics a valuable special collection in Optics was presented in 1934 in honor of Adolph Lomb by his brother and co-collector, Henry Charles Lomb. This collection was received through the good offices of James Powell Cocke Southall, Professor of Physics at Columbia University, a warm friend of the Lomb brothers and of the University of Virginia, of which he was an alumnus. At the time of his retirement from active teaching, Professor Southall presented many of his own books to the University of Virginia Library. A fund to make additions to the Lomb Optical Collection possible was contributed by Dr. Lincoln Milton Polan of the Zenith Optical Company and by a group of seven other companies engaged in the manufacture of optical instruments. In Biology two collections of outstanding value had been received in this period. One was of material in Ornithology, donated by Joseph Harvey Riley, for forty-five years a member of the Staff of the United States National Museum, a devoted scientist whose recognized distinction far out-ran his own modest claims. The other was a collection on Darwinian Evolution, gathered over a long period of years by Paul Bandler Victorius, a bookdealer, some of whose quests after missing editions approached the excitement of detective fiction. This collection was purchased for the University Library by an anonymous—and very generous—donor. The University's material in Geology, which like that in general Biology was of only moderate strength, had been aided in 1939 by a money contribution from Sumner Welles, then Under Secretary of State—a pleasing example of constructive interest in Geopolitics.

In the course of this period the University of Virginia organized three experiment stations away from Charlottesville: the Blandy Experimental Farm in Clarke County in northern Virginia, the Mountain Lake Biological Station in Giles County in southwestern Virginia, and the Seward Forest in Brunswick County in the southeastern part of the State. For the advanced work being conducted at those stations books were regularly lent from the University Library; and at the Mountain Lake station a special pamphlet collection had been organized. At each station what amounted to a small laboratory library had been assembled, but these had not by 1950 been linked with the centralized library administration. The books of Alfred Akerman, the first Director of Seward Forest, had in 1934 been presented to the collection in Forestry at the general library in Charlottesville.

One flourishing collection located away from Charlottesville, a complete college library which in 1950 numbered 80,016 volumes, had come under the aegis of the University of Virginia in 1944, as the result of an action of the General Assembly towards the solution of the long discussed question of the admission of women students. That question had arisen in the 1890's, had become a controversial issue during the administration of President Alderman, and had reached partial settlement in 1920 when women were permitted to attend the graduate and professional schools of the University on the same basis as men students. The act of 1944 had authorized the transformation of the State Teachers' College at Fredericksburg into a coordinate liberal arts college for women as Mary Washington College of the University of Virginia, bringing the College officially under an enlarged Board of Visitors, with the President of the University designated as Chancellor. Under the alert administration of Dr. Carrol Hunter Quenzel, who had become Librarian in 1943, this college collection, housed in the E. Lee Trinkle library building which had been completed in 1941, had made rapid progress in size and efficiency. The distance between Charlottesville and Fredericksburg had prevented common on-campus use; and the Mary Washington collection has not been included in the University totals. In other ways the cooperation between these two library centers had been close.

What had been in 1925 a small working collection of three or four thousand volumes in Engineering had by 1950 increased to 17,079 catalogued volumes. Money contributions by the Alumni and an endowment fund established by Mr. Jack Chrysler in memory of his father, Walter Percy Chrysler, and secured through the interest of Mr. Harcourt Parrish, had been added to the Barksdale endowment for Engineering and were facilitating further expansion. The main lines of curriculum interest were in Chemical, Civil, Electrical, and Mechanical Engineering, with research undertakings in Aeronautical Engineering, Highway Investigation, and Water Resources—a range that called for extensive library support. The acquisition in 1950 of the Thomas Winthrop Streeter collection on southern railways had immediately proved of research importance. This Streeter collection was located in the Rare Book Division of the Alderman Library.

Coincident with the opening of the new library building in 1938 and the coming of the McGregor gift had been the acquisition, made possible by a grant from the Alumni

Board of Trustees, of the Edward Lee Stone collection on the development of the printing art—volumes which, as the special bookplate appropriately stated, "mirror the personality of him who brought them together."

By 1950, therefore, there had been definite advance as a college library, in support of undergraduate instruction; and as a research library there had emerged a score or so of points of strength, scattered widely over the map of learning. Something had been accomplished in the effort to improve the facilities for productive scholarship in the southern area of the United States; though by the test afforded by the so-called "Farmington Plan"—that extraordinary cooperative effort towards American acquisition of foreign publications which was conceived by an intrepid little group meeting in October 1942 at Farmington, Connecticut—by that test the University of Virginia Library was still short of the possibility of assuming any but the meagerest share. The resolution adopted by the Faculty Library Committee in 1940—"that the University Library is unable to undertake unlimited acceptance of printed and manuscript materials"—was not merely in frank realization of the necessity for selection among acquisitions but it was also in support of a policy of cooperative and not competitive efforts. That resolution envisaged the elevation and extension, as this Library's contribution to research, of several crests rising above an adequate foundation of essential materials in all fields, with emphasis on a thoroughly equipped reference collection. What had already been achieved in the high points had depended upon gifts. For the foundation plateau and the reference material highways there was need of greater general funds than had yet been obtained. Of President Alderman's two millions of dollars, one had been secured for the "great library building." The million for "an adequate endowment" was in 1950 still being sought.

6. THE STAFF

Thus the library effort during 1925-1950 struggled upward by several paths: towards a general library buildng, towards an adequate catalogue, towards a storehouse of books that would facilitate research as well as undergraduate studies. Yet those goals were but means, not the desired end. It was the fourth effort, the development of a skilled and cooperative Staff, that would most directly affect the quality of the service that was the central purpose of this period of reorganization. It was in this matter of a Staff that the greatest measure of success had been achieved.

In July 1925 there had been seven full time members and one student part time assistant in the Library Staffs. The indications at that time were that librarianship had been offering little appeal to graduates of the University of Virginia. At the end of June 1950 there were sixty-six full time members and forty-five student or other part time assistants in the Library Staffs. Moreover all of the heads of divisions in the general library who had received appointment during those twenty-five years had previously been students at the University; and all of them had at one time or another since their appointments received tempting offers of library positions elsewhere. The quality of technical skill had become high, the contributions of original and constructive ideas had been outstanding, and many letters in the library files bore tribute to the range and spirit of the services that had been rendered. The story of what happened is a pleasant one. But it is too long to be told here. Some isolated bits must suffice.

One bit has already been told—the manner in which a small group of Cataloguers applied to a huge task the formula of interest and patience and good cheer; and how the opportunity afforded by the Humanities Fund had been utilized for an early increase of that Cataloguing Staff.

Another bit appropriately began with Christmas. During the Christmas holidays of 1928, an undergraduate, who had been reported to the new Librarian as having capably performed an odd job or two for the Library at the Rotunda, was engaged to undertake one of the many special pieces of work that then impeded the very entrance to any paths towards progress. What that task was has been forgotten—but not the speed, accuracy, and completeness of the performance. It was not long before a regular part time assistantship had been found for that student. It so happened that he had two undergraduate friends—a sort of Three Musketeer group. The two were intrigued by this new occupation of their comrade, even as Tom Sawyer's mates discovered that whitewashing a fence had unsuspected glamor. In a few months they also were members of the Student Library Staff. It was good fortune for the new Librarian. For these three student assistants, being at the same time users of the Library and workers behind the scenes, had acquired a double point of view. Since they were endowed with both curiosity and imagination, they readily grasped the meaning of plans intended to make library work yield greater dividends in library service. They also found that their modestly ventured suggestions were being considered and not infrequently adopted. There had been no thought in their minds of library business as a permanent occupation; and the full time positions that were offered them when they graduated meant to them at first merely a means for financing graduate study. But their own contributions to an expanding programme tied them to that programme by making it their own. That it was their own needs no proof except their names. The student who started this by working through his Christmas holidays was John Wyllie, Curator of Rare Books and of the Mc-Gregor Library; and his two friends were Randolph Church, Virginia State Librarian, and Jack Dalton, eleventh Librarian of the University of Virginia.

Another bit had only indirect effect on the permanent Staff. But the utilization of depression means in order to clean up the 1927 list of undone jobs had undoubted value for morale. In 1933 federal emergency relief funds became available for library work by students and others. Those were the funds which helped to coin a language of abbreviations: CWA, FERA, NYA, WPA. At the University of Virginia they were for the most part administered by Charles Henry Kauffmann, Director of Student Help; and his enthusiastic support of the library undertakings made his contribution to the reorganization programme vitally effective. On its part, the library administration was able to present a score or more of worthwhile projects that demanded concentrated effort and in some cases had instructional and apprenticeship values. From the number employed—on the peak year there were 156 library appointees—there was an unrivalled opportunity to select library minded workers for regular student assistantships. It is true that the task of training and supervising ever-changing groups of part time workers necessarily drew regular members of the Staff off from their routine duties; and that an equal amount of money expended on full time and skilled assistants might have produced more effective results. But for the Library's clean-up jobs these emergency funds proved a veritable gift horse. For the ten years 1933 to 1943, during which the funds were available, the records for all the University Libraries totalled 1,119 individuals who performed 277,081 hours of work and received $112,730.12 in wages.

Two developments in the staff situation came from acts of the General Assembly of Virginia which affected the libraries of all state supported institutions. The Certification Law, which went into operation on 1 July 1937, established professional standards for the more responsible library positions. This law applied also to the libraries of

Engineering, Law, and Medical Library Reading Rooms

A

CATALOGUE

OF THE

LIBRARY

OF THE

UNIVERSITY OF VIRGINIA,

ARRANGED ALPHABETICALLY

UNDER DIFFERENT HEADS, WITH THE NUMBER AND SIZE OF
THE VOLUMES OF EACH WORK, AND ITS EDITION SPECIFIED.

ALSO,

A NOTICE OF SUCH DONATIONS OF BOOKS AS HAVE BEEN
MADE TO THE UNIVERSITY.

PUBLISHED BY GILMER, DAVIS, & CO.
CHARLOTTESVILLE, VA.

1828.

THE BYRD LIBRARY

A Collection of Virginiana, in the Library of the University of Virginia,
founded on the Alfred Henry Byrd Gift

COMPILED BY
JOHN S. PATTON, Librarian
with a prefatory note by Robert Lewis Harrison

Charlottesville, Va.
The University of Virginia Press
1914

GENERAL INDEX
ANNUAL REPORTS ON
HISTORICAL COLLECTIONS
UNIVERSITY OF VIRGINIA LIBRARY

VOLS. XVI-XX, 1946-1950

UNIVERSITY OF VIRGINIA
CHARLOTTESVILLE
1952

THE JEFFERSON PAPERS
OF THE
UNIVERSITY OF VIRGINIA

A CALENDAR COMPILED BY
CONSTANCE E. THURLOW & FRANCIS L. BERKELEY, JR.

WITH AN APPENDED ESSAY BY HELEN D. BULLOCK ON THE
PAPERS OF THOMAS JEFFERSON

University of Virginia Bibliographical Series
Number Eight

Published by the University of Virginia Library
Charlottesville, Virginia

With Assistance from the Research Council of the
Richmond Area University Center

1950

Some Library Publications

political subdivisions exceeding 5,000 in population. It was the result of several years of effort by the Virginia Library Association, in which effort several members of the Staff of the University of Virginia Library took an active part; and on the three member State Board of Certification for Librarians Mr. Clemons and Mr. Dalton in succession received appointments from the Governor. Of the sixty-six full time members of the Staffs of the University Libraries in 1950, twenty-six had qualified for professional status. By the State Personnel Act, which went into effect 1 July 1942, both professional and non-professional members of Library Staffs were, along with the majority of other employees of the State, graded for salary standards. Acting as consultants in the matter of library grading, members of the Staff of the University of Virginia Library had a part in this development also. The Personnel Act did much to solve the vexed problem of inequalities in salaries, and it also supplied the machinery for cost-of-living adjustments to which reference has earlier been made. Of course strict standardization presents its own problems. But by 1950 the understanding, patience, and loyalty of the Library Staff at the University of Virginia had won through to the reward of a comparatively satisfactory situation, there being both recognition of the professional status of library work and of its appropriate compensation. There was ample cause for the satisfaction of the University and of the State also. For the later years had brought evidence of a widespread impression that the Staff of the University of Virginia Library was the peer of any in the country.

At the Alderman Library the introduction of research services, while the functions of a college library were at the same time being maintained, had brought about conditions for specialization. The small Staff of 1925 had been performing the duties pertaining to the purchase, cataloguing, and circulation of books. As expanded, these functions had developed into the separately organized Acquisitions, Preparations, and Circulation Divisions. To those had, in the 1925-1950 period, been added the Reference and Rare Book and Manuscript Divisions, making five in all. It was a planned development. But in a background of economic and political crises, the growth had necessarily been opportunistic and poorly balanced. It had been conditioned by acute pressures at certain points and relief had come through fortuitous circumstances. Such had been the expansion of the Preparations Division because of the cataloguing campaign, and of the Rare Book and Manuscript Division because of the rapid increase of manuscripts and rare books. It was not until toward the close of the period that there had been adequate manning of the Acquisitions and Reference Divisions; and further adjustments upward were definitely on the programme for the second quarter of the Library's second hundred years.

Partly to offset the isolation disadvantages of specialization, it had been deemed wise, after the move into the Alderman Library building, to create a representative body of the Library Staffs in order that information concerning local library activities might be made available to all. The purpose being the spread of information, not executive action, the meetings could be kept within time limits, committee discussions and administrative conclusions coming to this group merely as reports. With a touch of persiflage, this body had been dubbed the Board of Aldermen. Its meetings were at first held fortnightly and afterwards monthly; and in course of time the minutes of its meetings were made available for all members of the Library Staffs and for the members of the Faculty Library Committee. The Board of Aldermen thus became a sort of reportorial body, and its minutes a bulletin of current information.

Since the individuals composing this group were carrying the major part of the executive responsibilities of the

University of Virginia Libraries, brief personal statements will be given concerning the personnel of the Board as constituted at the end of this period. It seems the more fitting that this be done because at that stage those individual responsibilities would have compared not unfavorably with those borne by the first nine Librarians.

The three department libraries were represented by their Librarians, Miss Frances Farmer for the Law Library, Miss Elizabeth Frances Adkins for the Medical Library, and Miss Nellie Imogene Copps for the Engineering Library.

Miss Farmer held B.A. and LL.B. degrees from the University of Richmond, where she had been Law Librarian prior to her appointment in 1942 as Executive Secretary of the Law Library Committee at the University of Virginia. In the latter position she had organized and supervised the cataloguing of the law collection. Becoming Law Librarian in 1945, she had extended the usefulness of the Law Library by offering reference and other services to the alumni and to the legal profession in general. She had, for example, arranged for the cataloguing of the State Law Library in Richmond. She had also taken over the instruction in the required course in Legal Bibliography, the manual for that course having as joint authors Miss Farmer and Judge Malcolm Ray Doubles. She was a member of various legal societies, and was Secretary of the American Association of Law Librarians.

Miss Adkins had been a college student at Hollins College and the University of Virginia, and held a B.S. degree from the University of Virginia and a B.A. in Library Science from the University of North Carolina. Prior to becoming Medical Librarian in 1947, she had had a varied experience; as a high school librarian in Alexandria, Virginia, as assistant in a legislative reference library in Baltimore, as a cataloguer at the University of Virginia and at the University of North Carolina, at the latter being in charge of

Latin American materials, and as a war service librarian at Fort Monroe, Virginia.

By way of an aside, it may be noted that, while Miss Farmer had been preceded as Law Librarian by Mrs. Graves who had a notably long term of service, extending from 1912 to 1945, and while Miss Copps had been the first to hold the post of Engineering Librarian as a full time position, there had been eight Medical Librarians between the removal of that Library from the Rotunda to the new medical buildings in 1929 and the appointment of Miss Adkins. The eight had been Mrs. Margaret Otto, Mrs. Anne Ashhurst Gwathmey, Miss Caroline Hill Davis (formerly of the Columbia University Library), Mrs. Dora Mitchell Browning, Mrs. Miriam Thomas Buchanan, Miss Anne Lewis Morris, Miss Mary Elizabeth Mayo, and Miss Mabel Cook Wyllie (sister of the Curator of the McGregor Library). The difference at the Medical Library had arisen from the effect of marriage upon tenure of office. Four on that list had departed when their husbands took positions away from Charlottesville, and three (in a row) had resigned to become married. For clarification it should perhaps be added that only two of the seven husbands were doctors of medicine.

Miss Copps had taken courses at Stratford College, Columbia, and the University of Virginia. She had become Engineering Librarian in 1945. For a considerable period prior to 1942 the engineering collection had been under the supervision of Professor Charles Henderson, later to become Dean. In 1942 Professor Edwin Claire McClintock, Jr., had assumed the supervision; and after the appointment of Miss Copps, he became Chairman of the Engineering Faculty Library Committee. Miss Copps had previously held the post of Extension Librarian in an interesting attempt on the part of the University of Virginia to cooperate with the Virginia State Library in giving public library service to counties in the State where no local libraries were available. In accordance with the understanding when that cooperation began in 1928, as soon as the state appropriations to the Extension Division of the State Library seemed to be sufficient to enable that Division to take over the entire responsibility for fiction material, the University's part became limited to the regular service of the Reference Division of the Alderman Library. It was at that point that Miss Copps had been transferred to the much needed full time post of Engineering Librarian.

The other members of the Board of Aldermen were drawn from the Staff of the General Library.

Miss Mary Louise Dinwiddie had been a member of the General Library Staff since 1911 and had been Assistant Librarian since 1912. She had taken courses at the University of Virginia, and in 1913 she had attended a summer course in Library Science at Columbia University. Her store of information from the past had been valuable in phases of the clean-up job, an example being her supervision of a squad of federal relief workers in the laborious task of handling the accumulation of thousands of dusty volumes strewn over the dome floor of the Rotunda. Such services were carried over into the supervision of the exchange and binding routines, and into the assembling, arranging, and storing of stocks of the various university publications. The hours spent in this last project gave promise of a saving of time for many years after 1950, the date of her retirement. Miss Dinwiddie had been prominent in the activities of the Virginia Library Association; and during World War II she had been Director for Virginia of the collecting of books for the soldiers and sailors.

As has been noted, the major problem of cataloguing had resulted in an increase of the Staff of the Preparations Division somewhat out of proportion to the other Divisions. As an early attempt to facilitate the adoption of the Library of Congress classification by appointing as over-all super-visor an expert Cataloguer who was retiring from the Library of Congress had failed, because of the prolonged illness of that expert, the four senior members of the Cataloguing Staff had joined forces to master the problems involved, and gradually, with generously granted counsel from the Library of Congress, had worked out a manual of procedure. The four consequently became known as the Manual Committee. The Library had benefited greatly by having the continuous services of these four during the prolonged special cataloguing campaign. It had seemed appropriate, therefore, that all four be members of the Board of Aldermen, more especially since each had taken charge of a section of the general task. The division of the responsibility had been the result of a voluntary arrange-ment by the four concerned—and it had been indicative of the spirit that characterized that undertaking that the selection of types of work had been along lines of interest and recognized difficulty, not along lines of least resistance.

Mrs. Grigsby Farrar Bailey (Mrs. Thomas Dallas Bailey) had studied at the Packer Collegiate Institute in Brooklyn and at the Brooklyn Public Library Training School. She had been in charge of circulation at the Rotunda during the session of 1922-1923, had been Acting Librarian of the Charlottesville Public Library for the years 1923 to 1925, and had returned to the University of Virginia Library as Cataloguer in 1926. In the later division of the work she had elected to take charge of serial catalogu-ing—and thus incidentally became one of the noble band of contributors to the successive *Union Lists of Serials*.

Miss Marjorie Dunham Carver had begun her connec-tion with the Library in 1920 as Secretary to the Librarian but had almost immediately been transferred to a special position as Secretary to the General Chairman of the Cen-tennial Committee, a post she held for two years. In 1922 she had returned to the Library, as Secretary (until 1927) and as Special Cataloguer. She had been placed in charge of the recataloguing group in 1929, and it was she who had led that group in the excursion to Minor Hall and in the preparation of the "nucleus library." After the moving into the Alderman Library building, Miss Carver had continued in charge of special cataloguing projects. One of those had been the development of the pamphlet collection at Mountain Lake. Early in the process of acquiring this varied experience, Miss Carver had profited from the University's extension courses in Library Science.

Miss Lucy Trimble Clark had taken summer courses at the University of Virginia and had had some experience in teaching, in the work of the University Press, and in the circulation service of the Charlottesville Public Library before becoming in 1924 an assistant in circulation at the University of Virginia Library. In 1927 she had transferred to cataloguing. Work on books for which there was no prospect of obtaining Library of Congress printed cards had appealed to her, and she went on to train herself in the intricacies of rare book cataloguing, thus fitting her efforts into the programme for developing a research library. Appropriate recognition of her achievements had come in her election as a member of the Council of the University of Virginia Bibliographical Society.

Miss Olive Dickinson Clark had studied at Roanoke College and at Sweet Briar. At the University of Virginia Library she had started in 1923 as assistant in circulation, and had been in charge of circulation from 1924 to 1928. She had, however, felt the appeal of the cataloguing type of library work and in 1928 followed her sister into what was to become the Preparations Division. In the work of that Division Miss Olive Clark had assumed the responsibility for new cataloguing—that is, of books which, whatever their date of publication, were new to the University Library, and for which Library of Congress printed cards were available. To her had come also the responsibility for cataloguing the music collection.

Miss Louise Savage, the Acquisitions Librarian, had joined the Staff in 1930. It had been an act of faith—she had had such confidence in the probable developments at the University of Virginia Library that to take charge of its acquisitions duties she had at considerable financial sacrifice left a post as Librarian and Dean of Women at Elon College in North Carolina. Her earlier college studies had had to be interrupted by periods of teaching—her teaching subjects had been mathematics and science—but two years at the Randolph Macon Woman's College and some summer quarters at the University of Virginia had gained for her a degree of B.S. from the latter. In 1932-1933, while on leave from the acquisitions position, she had acquired also a B.S. in Library Science at the George Peabody College for Teachers in Nashville. One of the outstanding achievements of this whole period of the Library's history had been her successful effort during the second world war—specifically from September 1942 through December 1945—to carry the double responsibilities of the Acquisitions and of the Rare Book and Manuscript Divisions. As for the Acquisitions Division, which had been continuously in her charge from 1930, except for the session spent in Nashville, when Miss Bertha Cornelia Deane had capably substituted, that Division had been developed to a notable degree in extent, in efficiency, and in economy in the business operations of the library administration. Miss Savage's services had meantime been increasingly in demand from outside organizations—library, educational, bibliographical, social, religious —and it had been noticeable that none of the tasks for which her aid had been sought had fitted into the classification of sinecures. Her recreations also had been active—hunting, fishing, gardening, and spotting air planes.

Miss Helena Craig Koiner, who was in 1950 Senior Assistant in the Acquisitions Division, had been Secretary to the Librarian when the meetings of the Board of Aldermen had been started, and she had shared with Miss Carver the secretarial duties for the Board. In 1942, at the time when Miss Savage had taken on the rare book and manuscript responsibilities along with those of acquisitions, Miss Koiner had been transferred to the Acquisitions Division. She had taken college courses at the Stonewall Jackson College in Abingdon, Virginia, at the University of Virginia, at Columbia University, and at the University of North Carolina, and she had taught in Virginia, Massachusetts, and China—a wide range of training and experience. In 1947 she and Miss Ruth Evelyn Byrd of the Rare Book and Manuscript Division had passed with distinction the Virginia State Board examinations for professional library certification.

Miss Roy Land, the Circulation Librarian, had, like Miss Savage, joined the Staff in 1930. Also as in Miss Savage's case, her college undergraduate work had necessarily been interrupted by teaching. She had completed the junior college course at Averett College in Danville, Virginia, had had a session at Westhampton College at the University of Richmond, and then had progressed to a B.S. degree at the University of Virginia. It was as a graduate student that she began part time work at the University of Virginia Library, her early assignments being in various phases of the library routines. Directly after gaining an M.S. degree in English—that was in 1931—she became a full time circulation assistant; and three years later she was promoted to head the circulation work, following the resignation of Miss Virginia Cloud Jacobs. The rapid extension of the circulation services after the removal to the Alderman Library building was under the leadership of Miss Land; and notwithstanding the increased burden of responsibilities, she maintained to a degree widely and favorably recognized the quality of those services to the Library's public. In 1942-1943 a special grant from the General Education Board enabled her to spend a session in library study at the University of Michigan, her post at the Alderman Library being admirably carried by Miss Elizabeth Dillard Waterman. At Ann Arbor Miss Land made a distinguished record and added the degree of B.A. in Library Science to her collection. Meantime she had interested herself in the University's courses in dramatic art, and, particularly in the decade from 1929 to 1939, had taken leading parts in many of the productions of the Virginia Players. She had also been an organizer of the Extension Division's Bureau of School and Community Drama. That her ability as an organizer and speaker had been widely recognized had been evidenced by the calls upon her services by social groups and various library and literary organizations.

From the Board of Aldermen was to come the eleventh Librarian; and the next chapter in the history of the University of Virginia Library, beginning with July 1950, will be, using the Roman formula for Consuls, in the librarianship of Jack Dalton. With Jack Preston Dalton the practice of appointing an alumnus of the University to the library post was to be resumed. He had begun his college course at the Virginia Polytechnic Institute, but his B.S. and M.S. degrees had been gained at the University of Virginia. During the four sessions from 1930 to 1934 he had been an Instructor in English at the Virginia Polytechnic Institute, and he had seemed well on his way to a professorship in that subject when he was persuaded to return to the Rotunda to succeed Randolph Warner Church as Assistant Reference Librarian, Mr. Church moving on to Richmond to become Assistant State Librarian. During 1935-1936 Mr. Dalton studied Library Science at the University of Michigan on a special grant from the

General Education Board—and thus had opportunity to observe in Dr. William Warner Bishop how wide a range of possibilities there could be in constructive library leadership. During his absence at the University of Michigan, the expanding reference services had been ably performed by Anthony Vincent Shea, Jr., a graduate student who, unfortunately for the library profession, was not sufficiently attracted to make library service his life work. On Mr. Dalton's return in 1936, his position had been given the full title of Reference Librarian; and during the years immediately following, Mr. Dalton had employed his trained judgment in the selection of material appropriate for a university reference collection. In 1942 he was promoted to Associate Librarian, while retaining the direction of the Reference Division; and from that date, to him had gradually been entrusted the chief responsibility for state, regional, and national library relationships. Another grant from the General Education Board in 1949 had enabled him to make a nationwide study of postwar developments in library techniques and administration. It is doubtful if many University Librarians on their first assumption of that post have been equally well equipped—or have been as capable of profiting by that equipment.

Francis Lewis Berkeley, Jr., Curator of Manuscripts and University Archivist, had in 1945 returned from war service to continue the various phases of the work which had been begun by Dr. Lester J. Cappon. His postwar activities as collector of manuscripts had been one of the prime causes of the urgent need in 1950 of an extension of the library building; and his creation and performance of editorial opportunities had done much to expand the usefulness of the manuscript collection. Previous to his enlistment in the Navy in 1942 he had amply proved his fitness for a type of library service that would undoubtedly have met with the warm approval of Mr. Jefferson. He had taken a B.S. degree at the University of Virginia in 1934 and an M.A. in History in 1940. He had been an Assistant in English at the University, he had taught school in Gloucester County and in the City of Roanoke, and in the summers of 1933 and 1934 he had come to the attention of the library administration through his performance of the duties of an assistant in connection with the Virginia Collection. At the time of the removal into the new building in 1938, Mr. Berkeley had been wooed from teaching to become Senior Assistant in Charge of Manuscripts; and from October 1941 to September 1942 he had served as Acting Director of Rare Books and Manuscripts and Acting Curator of the McGregor Library.

As for his war service, it was in the Navy and in two parts. As Ensign and Lieutenant Junior Grade he had been in the Naval Armed Guard, and the operations in which he took part had penetrated into all the naval war theatres. As Lieutenant he had been assigned to the Amphibious Forces, and he had been in command of LSM 171 during the later stages of the operations in the Pacific—facing Japanese Kamikaze planes and the Fifth of June Typhoon with equal success. After discharge from active duty in October 1945 he had continued in the Naval Reserve and has since then been promoted to Lieutenant Commander.

In 1950 John Cook Wyllie was Curator of Rare Books and Curator of the McGregor Library. We have seen that his regular connection with the University of Virginia Library had begun during the 1928 Christmas holidays. A concise statement is given of the steps between those two dates. This is a factual statement. Such a record is peculiarly inadequate, because the material for a true biography of Mr. Wyllie would be ideas. To a limited degree it may be possible for the reader to catch the glimmering of such part of the story of ideas as lay behind these particular facts.

Mr. Wyllie received the B.A. degree from the University

of Virginia in June 1929. He was Assistant Reference Librarian from 1929 to 1933. It was "Assistant" merely because it was deemed wise to reserve the full title of Reference Librarian until the infant Reference Division could be more adequately developed. During 1933-1934 he was on leave for an adventure in tramp travel in Europe, special attention being given to libraries, binderies, and booksellers. On his return he became Curator of the Virginia Collection, holding that office from 1934 to 1938. Meantime in August 1936 he attended a University of Chicago Graduate Library School Institute, and in the summer of 1937 he did apprentice work under the master binders at the University of Michigan and at the New York Public Library. From 1938 to 1941 he was Director of the Rare Book and Manuscript Division and Curator of the McGregor Library; and during those years he virtually created the rare book collection by an exhaustive examination, book by book, of the collections in the general library. He was on leave of absence for war service from 1941 to 1945. It was when he came back at the end of 1945 that he took his present title. During the major part of 1948 he added to his regular duties, at the request of President Darden, the reorganization of the University Press. He took a leading part in the founding of the Albemarle County Historical Society and of the University of Virginia Bibliographical Society, and he had meanwhile been made a member of many other organizations, including the American Antiquarian Society. When the University of Virginia in 1948 conferred on him the Algernon Sydney Sullivan Award, the citation tersely stated that he had

in two decades performed a unique service both in peace and in war. His war experience extended to three continents, and to his acute embarrassment brought citations and medals from three nations. His services in peace have centered in the University Library, to the development of which he has contributed greatly;

199

but by his keen mind, indefatigable industry, and striking originality he has extended widely a wholesome influence for intellectual honesty and sturdy endeavor. The full story of his generous and self-sacrificing efforts is known to no one else, and has been forgotten by him.

Such in 1950, together with the tenth Librarian until his retirement on July first, was the membership of this representative group. There had also been in existence since 1942 a more comprehensive organization which had included all the members of the General Library Staff. This had delegated to a small, elected committee the arrangements for staff gatherings, the care and improvement of the staff room, and matters of social welfare, its financial basis being moderate annual dues. The natural tendency to over-organization had been successfully resisted, and this Staff Association had done much to engender and preserve a sense of family solidarity, which found its most lively expression, perhaps, in the annual Christmas parties.

Through the greater part of this period members of the Staff were also concerned, some as teachers and some as students, with the summer quarter and extension courses in Library Science. Such courses had been started by Librarian Patton in 1911, Miss Dinwiddie joining him as an Instructor in 1915. Requirements for the training of librarians in high schools had been established by the State Board of Education about 1928; there had consequently been a considerable increase in the number of students, and new courses had been added. At that time the Faculty Library Committee had given serious consideration to the advisability of establishing a degree-conferring Library School at the University of Virginia. The decision had been that the library science curriculum should be strengthened in order that the courses might be given credit towards the B.S. degree in Education; but that it seemed wise not to plan for a separate school offering a degree in Library Science.

Within the limits thus set, the effort had been successful. The courses—they had been increased to twelve by the summer of 1934—had been granted the desired credit, and they had been approved for teacher-librarians in high schools by the Virginia and Pennsylvania State Boards of Education and by the Southern Association for Colleges and Secondary Schools.

But during the second world war the summer courses in Library Science had quite innocently got caught in the line of fire from two directions. The reduced supply of teachers had compelled a relaxation of standardization requirements; and the three months summer period between regular sessions had been eliminated, shortening the normal four years of college to a continuous effort of thirty-six months and thereby crowding out a number of the customary summer quarter subjects. Since these library courses were thus without place and practically without students, they had quietly been numbered among the war victims. And when postwar action by the State Board of Education emphasized instruction for high school teacher-librarians at Madison College in Harrisonburg, the decision was accepted with equanimity.

As a matter of historical record, since the General Library had been involved in the administration of those library science courses, a faculty list is given for the 1925-1950 period. Miss Dinwiddie had continued as Instructor throughout the activation of the courses. Other members of the Staff who had offered instruction were Mr. Dalton (1936-1943, 1945, 1947), Miss Land (1947), Miss Savage (1931-1943, 1945, 1947), and Mr. Wyllie (1930-1932). To the Library Science Faculty had been added, for the summers indicated, Miss Lula Ocillee Andrews of the University of Virginia Extension Faculty (1929, 1930), Miss Georgia May Barrett of the University of Miami, Florida, Faculty (1929, 1930), Mr. Randolph Warner Church of the Virginia State Library (1933-1935), Miss Ethel Ruby Cundiff of the Faculty of the George Peabody College for Teachers, Nashville (1931-1933), Miss Mary Virginia Gaver, Librarian of the George Washington High School, Danville, Virginia (1934-1938), and Mrs. Dorothy Storey Watson, Supervisor of School Libraries, Roanoke, Virginia (1939-1943 and 1947).

To make the record complete, it should be added that during the 1930's some courses were offered outside those in the University's summer quarter. From 1931 to 1935 Miss Dinwiddie had conducted library science classes during the regular sessions at Mary Baldwin College in Staunton, Virginia; and in 1935-1936 she had been joined by Miss Savage in giving such instruction. For several scattered years these two and Mr. Wyllie had also been in charge of extension offerings in Library Science at Charlottesville, Lynchburg, Ashland, and Richmond.

7. PHASES OF THE LIBRARY SERVICE

In an earlier statement of the intent underlying the University Library's manuscript project, the expression was used, "to do the spade work for historical scholarship." Therein was both humility and aspiration. Thomas Jefferson recognized that there was range in library service. We have seen that to his mind the duties of a Librarian were simple, but that the possibilities of service mounted toward those of his own ministry as a counsellor to readers. As the Librarians of the first hundred years acquired age and experience, they increasingly enjoyed the privileges of contact with youth in a period of widening horizons. The gratifications of college librarianship carried over into the second hundred years; but to those had now been added new opportunities arising from the developing research functions of the University Library. There was evidence of the

THOMAS JEFFERSON *and his unknown brother* RANDOLPH

TWENTY-EIGHT LETTERS exchanged between Thomas and Randolph Jefferson concerning such homely matters as gerkins and parsneps, harness for a gigg, a spinning jenny, the education of a nephew and the death of a sister, some bougies from Dr. Caspar Wistar, shad and carp from James River, the mending of a watch, a shepherd bitch and her puppies, as well as divers other domestic subjects that interested the Sage of Monticello and his country-squire brother during the years 1807 to 1815; now for the first time put into print, together with an INTRODUCTION BY BERNARD MAYO.

THE TRACY W. McGREGOR LIBRARY
UNIVERSITY OF VIRGINIA, CHARLOTTESVILLE, 1942

MEMOIRS
of a
MONTICELLO SLAVE

AS DICTATED to Charles Campbell
in the 1840's by Isaac, one of
Thomas Jefferson's Slaves

EDITED BY
RAYFORD W. LOGAN
Professor of History
HOWARD UNIVERSITY

Published by the University of Virginia Press
for
THE TRACY W. McGREGOR LIBRARY
Charlottesville, Virginia
1951

McGregor Room and two McGregor publications

Th. Jefferson begs the Marquis de la Fayette's acceptance
of a copy of these Notes. the circumstances under which they
were written, & the talents of the writer, will account for their
errors and defects. the original was sent to Mons". de Mar-
-bois in December 1781. the desire of a friend to possess some
of the details they contain occasioned him to revise them
in the subsequent winter. the vices however of their original
composition were such as to forbid material amendment.
he now has a few copies printed with a design of offering
them to some of his friends, and to some estimable cha-
-racters beyond that line. a copy is presented to the
Marquis de la Fayette whose services to the American
Union in general, & to that member of it particularly
which is the subject of these Notes, & in that precise
point of time too to which they relate, entitle him to
this offering. to these considerations the writer
hopes he may be permitted to add his own perso-
-nal friendship & esteem for the Marquis. Un-
-willing to expose these sheets to the public eye
the writer begs the favor of the Marquis to put
them into the hands of no person, on whose care
and fidelity he cannot rely to guard them against
publication.

Jefferson Inscription to Lafayette in a Presentation Copy of the
First Edition of the *Notes on the State of Virginia*

quality of the Library Staff of the second century in its desire to discover and extend those new opportunities.

A good spirit in the normal service performed by a Library Staff is readily recognized. But there is no exact formula for its inculcation. Indeed there had been patent difficulties in the situation that prevailed in the University of Virginia Libraries, especially during the last decade of this 1925-1950 period. The open hours of the General Library and of the Engineering, Law, and Medical Libraries had been liberally extended. The Alderman Library was regularly open on weekdays for fifteen hours, from eight in the morning until eleven at night, except for a ten o'clock closing on Saturday nights; and the Sunday opening was from two in the afternoon until eleven at night—a weekly total of ninety-eight hours. Since the full time work week for a staff member was forty hours, this necessitated the selection of many assistants and the delegation to them of the responsibility for a willing and helpful service. It is a trite saying that a chain is as strong as its weakest link. The application to library service is obvious. The heads of the Divisions of the Library Staff had doubtless made such use of precept as might prove palatable. But it had obviously been their own examples that had been most potent; and in this matter of example, many other members of the Staff who have not been mentioned in this history had made notable contributions.

Other elements had affected the normal service of the University Library. In a period notorious for rapid changes in the personnel of American libraries, this Staff had benefited by a remarkable degree of continuity. Knowledge of the Library's resources that can be gained only by experience tends to expedite and expand the aid to students and scholars. Moreover encouragement had been given to staff members who showed a desire to keep in touch with the intellectual life of the University. One form that such encouragement had taken was an action by the Faculty Library Committee in 1944. The resolution read:

The Library Committee recognizes the desire on the part of several full time members of the Library Staff to improve their qualifications for service by taking university courses for which they are eligible; and it approves the policy of permitting the lecture hours for one such course each term to be counted as library time whenever this can be arranged without interfering with the library schedules.

Several members of the Staff, notably Miss Savage and Mr. Dalton, had volunteered assistance, outside of library hours, to non-professional members who wished to prepare for the State's library certification examinations; and for a considerable period Mr. Dalton had conducted an evening reading course for interested members of the Staff, the excitements of which had been readily carried over into the daytime routine contacts with books and readers.

The net result had been a responsive library service which had elicited much approbation. Commendation had been specific on the willingness—to use the Biblical phrase—to go the second mile, to take the initiative in the effort to be helpful. In the newly extended use of the Library for research endeavors there had been increased opportunities for thus giving positive force to the library service. To this end there had been experimentation in various ways. The ways were perhaps not novel. But there was some degree of novelty in their application to a Library, particularly to a rare book section of a Library. One element the experiments all seemed to have in common; namely, that there was much labor involved. The story of the phases of this library service might therefore be briefly described as compounded of some imagination, considerable courage, and very much hard work.

With the opening in 1949 of the exhibition gallery on the second floor of the Alderman Library, there had come

into use in that building four centers for display purposes—
an unusually abundant equipment for such uses. The
policy had been definitely away from permanent exhibits;
and the frequent changes, which the local press had been
encouraged to regard as newsworthy, had been steadily suggestive both of current interests and of the resources of the
Library. The range had been wide—from the works of a
local author or artist and from specimens from a student's
rare book gleanings or from a locally owned stamp collection to incunabula, illustrations of bookmaking, and editions and translations of the Bible; from material appropriate to Garden Week, the Music Festival, Founder's Day,
and Christmas to displays of French art, Japanese prints,
and Russian ikons; from homes and characters and events of
University and Virginia history to presidential campaigns
and the United Nations. Under Mr. Wyllie's supervision,
Miss Ruth Evelyn Byrd had made such exhibits her special
province; and Miss Land and her associates in the Circulation Division had steadily maintained in the entrance hall,
as temptations to borrowers, displays of books of current
interest.

There had been encouragement also to Professors giving
graduate courses, in which book materials were essential, to
hold occasional class meetings in the McGregor Room,
where rare editions pertaining to the subject matter of the
course could be examined and discussed. This had carried
into the humanities something of the value for science of
laboratory work and had helped to give meaning to such
vague terms as research and original sources. A development on a larger scale had been the occasional seminars in
modern prose and poetry which had been sponsored jointly
by the Schools of English and the Alderman Library. These
had been addressed by prominent literary figures and, with
admission by cards of invitation, had regularly attracted
audiences limited only by the capacity of the McGregor

Room. These had been called the McGregor Room Seminars. But beginning with 1951 they were to be known as the Peters Rushton Seminars, in memory of the young teacher and scholar who had taken a prominent part in their beginnings. For each of those meetings appropriate library exhibits had been prepared. Similar preparations had been made for the meetings in the McGregor Room of the University of Virginia Bibliographical Society, that society being a development from bibliographical interests which had found a congenial center in the Library's Rare Book and Manuscript Division. Another organization which had had its origin in a pooling of interests in local historical matters had been the Albemarle County Historical Society. Both the Bibliographical Society and the Historical Society had had their birthplaces in this Library, but the resulting membership had in each case extended well beyond the immediate university community. Thus, in addition to its primary function of affording intensive aid to research scholars, the Library had found indirect means for stimulating and extending literary and historical interests.

Moreover, both the Bibliographical and the Historical Societies had produced publications, the editorial work in each case centering in the Alderman Library. By 1950 there had appeared the first two volumes of *Studies in Bibliography,* the papers of the University of Virginia Bibliographical Society edited by Professor Fredson Bowers—a series which from its beginning was recognized as of marked distinction. By 1950 there had also been issued ten volumes of the *Papers of the Albemarle County Historical Society,* the first five edited by Archivist Cappon, the sixth to eighth by Dr. William Edwin Hemphill, and the last two by Mr. William Munford Ellis Rachal, Messrs. Hemphill and Rachal being members of the staff of the Virginia World War II History Commission, which then had its headquarters in the Alderman Library. At least two of the values of publications of a superior grade were illustrated by these series: they not only widened the recogniton of the services being rendered by these organizations, but they also proved an incentive to sustained effort by the organizations themselves.

The value of publications as an active force in public relations had already been recognized at the University of Virginia Libraries, and in this 1925-1950 period there had been started three series emanating from the General Library, one series of unique character from the Law Library, and a number of special publications and of contributions to cooperative undertakings.

The Law Library publication, *The Reading Guide,* had student editors and student and faculty contributors and consisted of signed reviews of new books and of interesting old books that could be found in the library stacks, each issue containing also a selected bibliography on a subject of contemporary importance.

Of the Alderman Library group, the first in point of time had been the *Annual Reports of the Archivist,* later entitled *Reports on Historical Collections.* Of these, twenty had been issued by 1950. Two cumulative indexes, covering years one to fifteen and years sixteen to twenty, formed a ready guide to what could be found in the extensive manuscript collection. The second was the *University of Virginia Bibliographical Series,* which began in 1941 and had reached its ninth number in 1950. The eighth number was an especially impressive publication, *The Jefferson Papers of the University of Virginia,* this being a calendar compiled by Constance E. Thurlow and Francis L. Berkeley, Jr. As for the third series, the publications of the Tracy W. McGregor Library, that had been a direct attempt to create a wider stimulus service for the rare books of the McGregor collection. The eight publications which had been issued by 1950 had each presented the text of a rare item of source material found in the McGregor Library, with critical introductions and bibliographical apparatus prepared by authorities from this or other Universities. The McGregor publications had been designed and printed with care and had been distributed widely, especially among members of the Southern Historical Association.

Among the special publications were a folder descriptive of the McGregor Library and a McGregor Reading List in American History, the latter being an experiment in widening the possibilities for a more exact knowledge of national history. This reading list had been issued during the last session of this period, and a widespread demand for it had led to several reprintings.

Emphasis on the principle of cooperation, the principle which had been adopted at the outset of the endeavor to make historical materials available for scholarly research, had led to opportunities not a few. One was the arrangement with the Virginia State Library and with other Virginia libraries to divide the responsibility for preserving files of local newspapers. Towards this effort the newspaper publishers and editors had proved generously responsive. Archivist Cappon's *Virginia Newspapers: A Bibliography with Historical Introduction and Notes,* a volume of some 300 pages which was issued in 1936 as a monograph of the University's Institute for Research in the Social Sciences, and which recorded the files held in various libraries, was among the first fruits of the effort to add availability to preservation.

Another comprehensive cooperative project in which the University of Virginia Library was associated with the Library of Congress, the Virginia State Library, the William and Mary College Library, and the Library of the Virginia Historical Society, and for which Mr. Wyllie was General Editor, was the compilation and publication of localized sections of a *Virginia Imprint Series*. Preliminary checklists for three centers had been issued by 1950. This plan of procedure had proved of interest to several other States; and reports of University of Virginia Library holdings of their imprints were at the close of this period being supplied to somewhat similar projects in Maryland, Pennsylvania, and New Jersey.

Other cooperative undertakings in which this Library had a share may be listed briefly. Most of these were being handled in the office of the Rare Book and Manuscript Division, and several were just beginning in 1950. One, which has already been mentioned, was the complete representation in the Union Catalogue at the Library of Congress of cards for University of Virginia book holdings. Cards for this Library's holdings in Confederate imprints had begun to go to an extensive project being sponsored by the Athenaeum Library in Boston; cards for unofficial Confederate publications had been sent for an undertaking at the University of North Carolina; and a listing of this Library's collection of Confederate music had been included in an index in preparation by Mr. Richard Barksdale Harwell, Curator of Special Collections at Emory University in Georgia. The University of Virginia Library had been contributing to the continuation in process at Worcester, Massachusetts, of the great Evans *American Bibliography;* to a film inventory at Philadelphia; to the Florida Catalogue at Winter Park; to the inventory of seventeenth century English books in process at Yale University, under the editorship of Dr. Donald Goddard Wing; to the union list of American literary manuscripts to be edited by Dr. Joseph J. Jones of the University of Texas; to the supplement to the De Ricci-Wilson *Census of Mediaeval and Renaissance Manuscripts in the United States and Canada,* which is to be edited by Professor Christopher Urdahl Faye of the University of Illinois; and to the compilation of American holdings of entries in the

Pollard and Redgrave *Short Title Catalogue,* this last being an undertaking by Dr. William Warner Bishop of the University of Michigan. The University of Virginia was of course contributing whenever opportunity offered to the Princeton edition of the writings of Thomas Jefferson. Checklists which had been or were being compiled at the University of Virginia Library of material connected with John Randolph of Roanoke, James Madison, James Monroe, and John C. Calhoun were, at the close of this period, being considered as the possible bases for extensive future publication projects by the National Historical Publications Commission.

Mention of the Princeton edition of Jefferson's Works and of the Thurlow-Berkeley calendar of *Jefferson Papers of the University of Virginia* brings us to the special attention that had been given in this period to this Library's Founder. The Library had become an active collector of books by and about Thomas Jefferson, of the many editions of the *Notes on the State of Virginia* and of the *Manual of Parliamentary Practice,* of manuscript letters, of material of all sorts. One huge undertaking had been conceived early in this 1925-1950 period and had been steadily and resolutely carried out: a checklist arranged chronologically of all reported Jeffersonian texts, either in print or in manuscript, including letters to him as well as those written by him, the entries giving date, description, location, and ownership, and information concerning printed form. It was realized that this Jefferson checklist would be of impressive size—and eventually it reached an accumulation of well over 75,000 record slips. Mr. Wyllie, who had started this while he was Curator of the Virginia Collection, had made work on it a continuous order of the day; and though others assisted, this was essentially his creation. When he obtained leave of absence for war service in the month before the attack on Pearl Harbor, the results had become so extensive and so visibly a record of Thomas Jefferson's daily interests that the Library of Congress proposed that this checklist be published under the joint imprint of the two Libraries —thus once more linking the major and the minor institutional collections which owed their origin to the same distinguished Founder. The impact of the second world war compelled postponement of any such project, however desirable. When, following the Jefferson Bicentennial of 1943, the generous and patriotic proposals from the New York Times and the Princeton University Press and the availability as Editor of the superbly equipped Dr. Julian Parks Boyd presented the possibility of as complete an edition of the Jeffersonian writings as seemed humanly possible, the need for the publication of the checklist was, for the time at least, transferred into its immediate value as the effective means for a rapid but comprehensive survey of what would be involved in the proposed undertaking. Had there been any serious question about value in "spade work for historical scholarship," that doubt could at that point have been gratifyingly dismissed.

The Bicentennial had also been a harvest time for books and articles about Jefferson. The following list is by way of illustration. This is, however, a list of books only; and of the many books written about Thomas Jefferson during this period only those have been included to whose authors or editors the University of Virginia Library is known to have been able to render some assistance. What this list really illustrates is, therefore, one more benefit conferred on this Library by its Founder. For he was now, in his own person as it were, endowing this Library with the subject matter for an especially fruitful and rewarding phase of its service.

Abernethy, Thomas Perkins, editor. A Summary View of the Rights of British America, by Thomas Jefferson. New York, Scholars' Facsimiles & Reprints, 1943.

Betts, Edwin Morris, editor. Thomas Jefferson's Garden Book, 1766-1824. Philadelphia. American Philosophical Society, 1944.

Betts, Edwin Morris, and Perkins, Hazelhurst Bolton. Thomas Jefferson's Flower Garden at Monticello. Richmond, The Dietz Press, 1941.

Bullock, Helen Duprey. My Head and My Heart: A Little History of Thomas Jefferson and Maria Cosway. New York, Putnam, c1945.

Cometti, Elizabeth, editor. Jefferson's Ideas on a University Library: Letters from the Founder of the University of Virginia to a Boston Bookseller. Charlottesville, Tracy W. McGregor Library, 1950.

Davis, Richard Beale, editor. Correspondence of Thomas Jefferson and Francis Walker Gilmer, 1814-1826. Columbia, University of South Carolina Press, 1946.

Davis, Richard Beale. Francis Walker Gilmer: Life and Learning in Jefferson's Virginia. Richmond, The Dietz Press, 1939.

Foote, Henry Wilder, editor. The Life and Morals of Jesus of Nazareth Extracted Textually from the Gospels of Matthew, Mark, Luke, and John, by Thomas Jefferson. Boston, The Beacon Press, 1951.

Foote, Henry Wilder. Thomas Jefferson, Champion of Religious Freedom, Advocate of Christian Morals. Boston, The Beacon Press, 1947.

Kimball, Marie. Jefferson, the Road to Glory, 1743 to 1776. New York, Coward-McCann, c1943.

Kimball, Marie. Jefferson, War and Peace, 1776 to 1784. New York, Coward-McCann, c1947.

Kimball, Marie. Jefferson: The Scene of Europe, 1784 to 1789. New York, Coward-McCann, c1950.

Koch, Adrienne, and Peden, William, editors. The Life and Selected Writings of Thomas Jefferson. New York, The Modern Library, c1944.

Logan, Rayford W., editor. Memoirs of a Monticello Slave . . . Charlottesville, The Tracy W. McGregor Library, 1951.

Malone, Dumas. Jefferson the Virginian. Boston, Little, Brown and Company, 1948.

Malone, Dumas. Jefferson and the Rights of Man. Boston, Little, Brown and Company, 1951.

Mayo, Bernard, editor. Jefferson Himself: The Personal Narrative of a Many-Sided American. Boston, Houghton Mifflin Company, 1942.

Mayo, Bernard, editor. Thomas Jefferson and his Unknown Brother Randolph . . . Charlottesville, The Tracy W. McGregor Library, 1942.

Shepperson, Archibald Bolling. John Paradise and Lucy Ludwell of London and Williamsburg. Richmond, The Dietz Press, 1942.

So this attempt at a history of the University of Virginia Library has ended where it began—with Thomas Jefferson; and its first paragraph might now profitably be reread along with these concluding sentences. Many long years, sundry visible changes, and a few exciting moments have separated the beginning and the end. In essence, however, there are a similarity and a difference between the situation in 1825 and the situation in 1950 which afford present cause for encouragement and for sober thought.

The Founder's estimate of the importance for the University of the service of its Library had been notably high. The more recent advances had in a measure restored to the Library the place which Jefferson had envisioned for it. That restoration had helped to renew the forward urge which was implicit in Jefferson's intent. The year 1950 was therefore not an end, but merely a link in the annals of a fresh beginning. Herein was the stimulus for new hope.

There was reason also for sober thought. At its beginning in 1825 the books so carefully selected by Jefferson in his eighty-second year formed a solid and essential core for a well rounded university library. The additions to 1895 had been built on that firm foundation. Both foundation and superstructure had been in large part destroyed by the burning of the Rotunda. Since 1895 there had been assembled a vastly larger collection. But the order of the building process had been reversed. There was now much superstructure, but the firm foundation was still to be settled in. Attempts had been made from time to time to strengthen the edifice at its base. But this had been largely a process subjected to chance—to good fortune in gifts, to casual market offerings, to the moment's possession or lack of available general funds. It was at the end, not at the beginning, of the fifty-five years since 1895 of the University's new collection that the group of faculty representatives chosen as experts by the various Departments and Schools, for liaison with the Library's efforts at collection building, was settling down to create a want list of the significant works and monumental sets for each branch of learning. It is true that in the years that had elapsed since Jefferson's day more and broader fields of learning had been opened and surveyed, and that to establish what would now be a solid and essential core of university library materials would necessarily be a much larger undertaking. Yet in concept this purpose was identical with that performed by Jefferson when he compiled his list for the Boston bookseller. It was therefore a sobering thought as well as a stimulus to forward action that in 1950 some thirty experts, with a considerable degree of diffidence, had become engaged in a fundamental library undertaking which had in 1825 been achieved single-handed by the Sage of Monticello.

A FOOTNOTE

This story of the University of Virginia Library is being printed without footnotes. Among the reasons for this decision is the obvious fact that the greater part of the source material is in the form of archives which exist only at the University of Virginia. A typed form of the text with over a thousand notes has been deposited in the Alderman Library and is available at the Library for examination. Inquiries from outside of Charlottesville may be addressed to the Reference Librarian. So far as the printed form of the story is concerned, therefore, this is a footnote to end all footnotes.

SUNDRY ACKNOWLEDGMENTS

During the composition of this story the writer has received assistance from many sources. Individual acknowledgments have been made privately. It is a pleasure to add public expression to the following: to the Trustees of McGregor Fund for a grant which has safeguarded the opportunity for concentration on this project; to numerous members of the Staff of the University of Virginia Library for friendly and effective help at many stages; especially to Mrs. Lawrence Greaver for her patient struggle with the writer's handwriting in the typing of two complete versions of the text and of the index and one of the notes, and to the Library's Publication Committee, Miss Savage, Mr. Dalton, and Mr. Wyllie, for cheerful assumption of the tasks connected with publication and distribution; to Dr. Dumas Malone for his magnanimous response to the solicitation of the heads of the Library Staff that he write a Foreword (which the bewildered and embarrassed but deeply moved tenth librarian did not see until it was in its final form); to Mr. Francis L. Berkeley, Jr., Dr. Edwin Morris Betts, Mr. J. Malcolm Luck, Mr. Ralph Thompson, and the Meriden Gravure Company for both counsel and performance in the matter of the illustrations; to Mr. Charles Edward Moran, Jr., and Mr. Mark Rinker of the University of Virginia Press for their personal interest and tactful advice during the processes of printing; and last, and most emphatic, to Jeannie Jenkins Clemons for her unshaken faith and timely encouragements throughout the long months of her librarian husband's absorption in these memoirs of a Library. To her the completed book is dedicated.

216

Index

INDEX

MacIver, David Randall, 174.
McKeldin, James Reese, 126, 171.
McKim, Haslett, 66.
McReynolds, James Clark, 178.
Madison, Dolley, 24.
Madison, James, Statesman, 9, 20, 24, 25, 210.
Madison, James, President of College of William and Mary and Bishop, 9.
Madison College, 201.
Madison Endowment Fund, 23-25, 63.
Madison Hall, 79.
Madison Hall Library, 78, 79, 85, 86; references to student reading room that preceded the Madison Hall Library, 27, 51, 84.
Maine, Material on, 170.
Malone, Dumas, 140, 147, 212.
Manly, William Gwathmey, 174.
Manning, James, 3.
Manual Committee, 192.
Manuscript Collection, 23, 24, 48, 49, 67, 81, 155, 158, 161-167, 178.
Map Collection, 155, 161.
Martin, "Uncle" Henry, 54.
Martineau, Harriet, 13.
Mary Baldwin College, 202.
Mary Washington College, 181, 182.
Massey, Linton Reynolds, 172.
Mathematics, School of Applied, 41.
Mathematics Library, 51, 84, 85, 139.
Maupin, Socrates, 37.
Maury, James, 7.
Maxey, Kenneth Fuller, 179.
Mayo, Bernard, 212, 213.
Mayo, Mary Elizabeth, 190.
Mechanical Laboratory, 85, 150.
Medical Library, 26, 61, 66, 79, 85, 145, 149, 152, 179, 180, 189, 190, 203.
Medicine, Department of, 78.
Medicine, Material on, 179.
Meigs, William M., 45.
Mellor, Earl Godfrey, 173.
Memorial Welfare Association, 178.
Mercer, Charles Fenton, 176.
Metcalf, John Calvin, 87, 88, 110, 121, 126, 127, 135, 138, 143, 147, 158, 172.

Methods, School of, 71.
Mexico, Material on, 170.
Michigan, University of, 196, 197, 199, 210.
Microfilm Collection, 155, 173.
Microphotography, 142, 163.
Military Government, School of, 170.
Military Science, School of, 38.
Miller Fund, 42.
Minor, Ferrell Dabney, Jr., 83.
Minor, H. Dent, 178.
Minor, John Barbee, 34, 36, 109, 158, 178.
Minor, Raleigh Colston, 54, 84, 178.
Minor Hall, 71, 86, 149, 150, 193.
Monroe, James, 210.
Montgomery, Walter Alexander, 174.
Monticello, referred to as home of Jefferson, 11.
Moore, John Bassett, 80, 178.
Morgan, Wilbur Phelps, 79.
Morris, Anne Lewis, 190.
Morton, Richard Lee, 76.
Morton, William Wylie, 170.
Mountain Lake Biological Station, 181, 193.
Mulholland, Henry Bearden, 179.
Murray, Joseph, 2.
Music Library, 139, 145, 194.
Musicology, Material on, 175.

Nanking, 127.
National Historical Publications Commission, 210.
Navy, United States, 197, 198.
Neff, Eugene Ezra, 180.
Neff, John Henry, 179.
Negro, Books on, 83, 169.
New Jersey Imprint Series, 209.
New York Alumni, 65, 180.
New York Public Library, 199.
New York Times, 211.
Newcomb, John Lloyd, Second President of the University of Virginia, 87, 123, 135-137, 139, 140, 155, 158.
Newspapers, 131, 155, 208.
North Carolina, University of, 189, 195, 209.

224

and Schools, as Engineering, Department of.
Students, 14, 16, 27, 33-35, 41, 49, 54, 55, 77, 104, 124, 128.
Alumni, 26, 52, 53, 58, 62, 64, 65, 92, 137, 152, 158, 159, 177, 178, 180, 182. *See also* New York, Richmond, Washington Alumni.
Buildings, 1, 12-14, 26, 27, 36-39, 49-60, 71, 72, 79, 84-88, 109, 124, 126, 129, 130, 132-145, 149, 150. *See also* names of buildings, as Alderman Library Building.
Finances, 21, 22, 24, 42, 53, 62-64, 71, 77, 78, 83, 84, 88, 110, 118, 123, 124, 126, 135-138, 148, 155-158, 173, 174, 184. *See also* names of funds, as Humanities Fund. *See also* Depressions, Financial.
Readjuster Politics, 45, 46, 110, 115, 119.
Rotunda Fire, 27, 53-58, 85, 86, 89, 114, 118, 179.
Wars, 32-36, 39, 77, 97, 106, 108, 123, 124, 158, 159. *See also* War of 1861-1865, World War I, World War II.
Extramural Services, 32, 71, 73, 124, 157, 158, 163, 164, 187, 189-191, 200-202, 204, 206, 208-221.
General Conditions, 25, 26, 33-36, 40, 41, 77, 78, 102, 123, 124. *See also* Library, University of Virginia, Summaries of General Conditions.
Virginia Certification Law 186.
Virginia Collection, 167, 198, 199.
Virginia Historical Society, 166, 208.
Virginia Imprint Series, 209.
Virginia Intermont College, 82.
Virginia Library Association, 191.
Virginia Players, 196.
Virginia Polytechnic Institute, 196.
Virginia State Board of Education, 201.
Virginia State Law Library, 189.
Virginia State Library, 76, 166, 185, 190, 191, 196, 208.

Virginia State Personnel Act, 156, 187,
Walter, A. B., 99.
Walter, Albert Ulman, 170.
War of 1861-1865, 32-36, 39.
Washington, D. C., Alumni, 137.
Waterman, Elizabeth Dillard, 196.
Waterways, Material on, 171.
Watson, Dorothy Storey, 202.
Watts, Legh Richmond, 80.
Watts, Stephen Hurt, 179.
Webb, George Curle, 178.
Webb, Robert Henning, 110, 174.
Welles, Sumner, 181.
Wertenbaker, Charles Christian, 97.
Wertenbaker, Christian, 93.
Wertenbaker, Louisiana Madison Timberlake, 95.
Wertenbaker, Mary Grady, 93.
Wertenbaker, Thomas Grady, 97.
Wertenbaker, Thomas Jefferson, 197.
Wertenbaker, William, Second Librarian, 1, 5, 18, 21, 28-30, 39, 42-46, 49, 56, 93-101, 103, 105, 109, 115, 121, 145, 146, 154, 174.
Wertenbaker, William, eldest son of the Librarian, 97.
Westhampton College, 195.
Whistler, James Abbott McNeill, 6.
White, Stanford, 58, 72.
White, William Henry, 178.
Whitehead, Richard Henry, 179.
Wilke, Frederick Henry, 180.
William and Mary, College of, 3, 6, 7, 27, 60, 208.
Williams, Bruce, 171.
Willoughby, William Franklin, 171.
Wilson, James Southall, 82.
Wilson, Richard Henry, 173.
Wing, Daniel Goddard, 209.
Winston, William Aylett, Sixth Librarian, 45, 46, 110-113, 115.
Wisconsin, University of, 60.
Women Students, 181, 182.
Wood, Frederic Turnbull, 173.
Woodrow Wilson School of Foreign Affairs, 170.
Woolsey, John Munro, 178.

C O L O P H O N

This book was produced at the University
of Virginia Press under the supervision of
George Eager and of his successor, Charles
E. Moran, Jr. The basic design was planned
by John Cook Wyllie. The machine and
hand composition and the layout were the
work of Mark Rinker with assistance from
Jerold Grizzle and the presswork was by
William Travis. The collotype illustrations
were made by the Meriden Gravure Company of Connecticut under the supervision
of Harold Hugo. The binding was done by
the Charles H. Bohn Company of New
York under the supervision of Theodore
Tuck, using the Bancroft book cloth known
as Linen Finish 3350. The dust-jacket is
University of Virginia Press produced, from
halftones by Kiraly of Charlottesville. The
text type is Linotype Baskerville throughout,
12 on 13, with quotations and the footnote
10 on 11, and index 8 on 9. The display type
is Goudy Bold. The paper is Warren's 66,
70-pound, Antique Text. One thousand copies have been printed, of which this is

Number _945_